The Ochils

40 favourite Walks

The author and publisher have made every effort to ensure that the information in this publication is accurate, and accept no responsibility whatsoever for any loss, injury or inconvenience experienced by any person or persons whilst using this book.

published by
pocket mountains ltd
The Old Church, Annanside,
Moffat, Dumfries and Galloway DG10 9HB

ISBN: 978-1-907025-79-2

A catalogue record for this book is available from the British Library

Contains Ordnance Survey data © Crown copyright and database 2022 supported by out of copyright mapping 1945-1961

Printed by J Thomson Colour Printers, Glasgow

Introduction

The Ochils are a walker's paradise. Stretching northeast between the historic cities of Stirling and Perth and sandwiched between the River Forth and the Highland Boundary, the huge almost vertical southern escarpment is visible from across east Central Scotland and is particularly prominent from the M9 as it heads towards Stirling. Beyond Stirling, the M9 becomes the A9, rounding Dumyat and Sheriffmuir and veering back to the east towards Perth along the range's gentler northern side. The range was known to the ancient Celts of Central Scotland as *uchel* – 'The High Place'.

It is a name well deserved. Eleven of the hills are more than 610m (2000ft) high: Ben Cleuch, Andrew Gannel Hill, Ben Buck, King's Seat, Tarmangie, Whitewisp, The Law, Blairdenon, Ben Ever, Greenforet Hill and Innerdownie. Of these, all are classed as Donalds – hills over 2000ft with a drop of at least 50ft all around – except The Law, Ben Buck and Greenforet Hill. This guide covers all these summits.

Another five of the hills are classed as Marilyns – those with a prominence over 150m. These are: Ben Cleuch, Dumyat, Innerdouny Hill, Lendrick Hill and Steele's Knowe. All of these hills also feature in this guidebook.

But the hilltops are not the only focus of this guide. The magnificent narrow and steep-sided glens are covered, as are routes along the rivers that border

the Ochils: the Allan and the Devon.

At less than an hour's drive from both Glasgow and Edinburgh, these hills make for an easily accessible escape from the rigours of city life.

History

The Ochils offer a microcosm of human history, from prehistoric hunter-gatherers to the post-Industrial Revolution. Standing stones, ancient trackways and burial mounds show that these hills were important to our ancestors.

Hillforts at Craig Rossie, Dumyat, Glenearn, Abbey Craig, Abernethy and Tillicoultry demonstrate their defensive value, while Roman forts and roads around the north and west of the range track the progress of the army of Septimius Severus in its attempts to subdue the Caledonian tribes. Later fortifications include the medieval castles at Dollar, Glendevon, Gleneagles and Menstrie.

The remains of farmsteads and shielings bear witness to the historic agricultural practice of transhumance, where cattle were moved to higher pastures in summer, which died out in the 18th century when the Lowland clearances made way for sheep.

Perhaps the most significant event in the Ochils' history took place on Sheriffmuir, east of Dunblane, on 13 November 1715. As a result of the 1715 Uprising, the Jacobites, under the Earl of

Mar, held Perth. A small Government army, under the Duke of Argyll, was based at Stirling. The two armies met at Sheriffmuir. The battle stumbled to an end with no conclusive winner.

Later industrial progress saw the Hillfoots villages expand around the huge mills that sprang up to take advantage of the fast-moving burns that flowed down from the hills.

The natural environment

Seen from the south, the huge upland massif of the Ochils appears as one long escarpment, highest at its western end by Stirling and tapering down towards Perth in the east. The steep southern face drops suddenly down almost to sea level, with only the large flat plain of Clackmannanshire between it and the River Forth, which snakes across the Central Belt to Stirling.

The steep face is the result of the Ochil Fault, a major geological fault which, some 340 million years ago, pushed a bed of volcanic rock upwards. To this day, minor earthquakes can still sometimes be felt in the area.

The lava bed now forms a high and undulating plateau, with no prominent peaks – indeed, between Mickle Corum in the west and Innerdownie in the east it is possible to reach 16 named summits without dropping below 530m.

Over the intervening millennia, the south-flowing burns, aided by the retreating glaciers of the ice age, have cut deep, dramatic ravines, including Menstrie Glen, Alva Glen, the Silver Glen, Mill Glen and Dollar Glen, all of which extend high into the hills, providing access to the plateau. On the northern side, the hills are less dramatic, rolling gently down towards the flat plain of Strathearn.

The Ochils are home to some rare plant and animal species. They are one of only 10 places in the UK where the very rare sticky catchfly plant can be found. The Northern brown argus butterfly is another rare species that makes its home here. Less rare, mountain hare and red deer may be seen on the slopes, as well as the ubiquitous sheep.

Public transport

There are regular bus services to the start of many of the walks. Be aware that bus routes can change, so these should be checked before commencing your walk (www.travelinescotland.com).

The main railway line between Stirling and Perth passes up the west and northern sides of the Ochils, providing services to Bridge of Allan, Dunblane and Gleneagles (for Auchterarder).

There is no public transport through either Glen Devon or Dunning Glen.

How to use this guide

This guide contains 40 low-level and hill walks. The low-level walks are on good paths and tracks and are generally waymarked or are easy to follow.

For the hill walks, you should always

carry a map and compass and know how to use them. The requisite OS Explorer maps (366, 369, 370 and OL47) are noted in the text. Harvey's Superwalker XT25 'Ochil Hills' map is also recommended, as it shows several of the tracks and paths within this guide not found on the OS Explorer maps listed above.

A whistle and a headtorch are also advisable for hill walks, along with a few fully charged USB power packs, spare provisions and a first aid kit, just in case. Be prepared for shortened daylight hours in winter and for the challenges of poor weather at any time of year.

Walking conditions can change; wet weather can quickly turn an unsurfaced footpath into a quagmire and steeper slopes can become slippery with mud. Strong winds too, particularly on higher ground, can be dangerous.

Many walkers use Global Positioning Systems (GPS), but signals can be lost and phones can run out of power. GPS can show you where you are, but it cannot tell you where to go next in conditions of poor visibility.

Preparation for your walk begins at home. Choose a route that reflects the abilities of both you and those who will accompany you. Dress appropriately for the weather and the terrain: this is Scotland and carrying warm waterproof clothing is generally advisable, even if you don't think you'll need it. Comfortable waterproof walking shoes are fine for the lower-level walks. Good-quality walking boots are recommended for the hills, and walking poles are always handy, regardless of the terrain.

Access

The Land Reform (Scotland) Act of 2003 gives members of the public a right to access most Scottish land and inland waters, and landowners have a responsibility not to unreasonably prevent or deter access. However, key to the Act is that members of the public exercise their rights responsibly, as laid out in the Scottish Outdoor Access Code (www.outdooraccess-scotland.scot).

Take your litter home with you. Respect the environment and private property, and do not damage fences and crops. Close all gates behind you.

Dogs should be kept under strict control, particularly in the spring and early summer when they could disturb ground-nesting birds. Do not enter a field with your dog if there are lambs, calves or other young farm animals. If you enter a field where there are animals, keep your dog on a short lead and stay as far away from the animals as possible. If cattle become aggressive, keep calm, let your dog go, and take the shortest, safest route out of the field. It goes without saying that dog waste should not be left behind: bag it and bin it.

The Wallace Monument ▶

At their western end, the Ochils narrow down to a point at the most accessible and popular hill in the range, Dumyat. With the Wallace Monument standing sentinel on its summit, Abbey Craig forms one last small hill before the range descends into the plains of the River Forth around Stirling.

Dumyat's popularity is no doubt due to its proximity to both Stirling and the campus of Stirling University at the foot of the hill in Bridge of Allan. The bridge itself replaced a ford across the River Allan in 1520 and the town grew up around it, expanding rapidly when it became a renowned spa town during the hydropathic boom of the 19th century.

North of Bridge of Allan, the town of Dunblane was named for the 6th-century Irish St Blane, who became a bishop to the Picts. St Blane founded a church on the site of the present-day Dunblane Cathedral, dating from the 11th century.

The great wall of the Ochils and the Firth of Forth forced invading armies from the south towards Stirling. This is an area that has seen many historic battles, including the Battles of Stirling Bridge (1297), Bannockburn (1314) and Sauchieburn (1488). These sites can all be seen from the summit of Dumyat.

Within the hills themselves, the Battle of Dumyat, when Áedán mac Gabráin, King of the Scots of Dalriada, led a decisive victory over the Maeatae, took place around 570AD.

Nearly 1200 years later, a few miles to the north, the only major engagement of the 1715 Jacobite Rising took place on Sheriffmuir. Despite fielding one of the biggest Jacobite armies ever assembled, with twice as many troops as the Government forces, they had an inexperienced commander. By all accounts, the battle was a tumultuous affair with both sides claiming victory.

Bridge of Allan and Dunblane lie on the railway line which snakes its way around the northwest of the Ochils, and both are now commuter towns for Stirling and Perth.

Dunblane and the west

1 **The Abbey Craig Trail**   8
Explore the hilltop where one of
Scotland's greatest heroes gathered
his troops for battle

2 **Dumyat by the hill path**   10
Take the easy route to the top
of Dumyat

3 **Dumyat by Logie Kirk**   12
Witches await you on this enjoyable
climb to the summit of the most
popular hill in the Ochils

4 **The Darn Road**   14
The Romans and a literary great
have walked this traditional
route between Bridge of Allan
and Dunblane

5 **The Glen Road**   16
Take this old road from Dunblane
to Bridge of Allan through a
picturesque glen

6 **Blairdenon**   18
Climb to the highest and most
remote point in the western Ochils
on this circular route

7 **The Battle of Sheriffmuir**   20
Head out of Dunblane to the
location of the most important
battle of the 1715 Jacobite Rising

8 **Dunblane to Ashfield**   22
Follow the River Allan from
Dunblane to the historic factory
village of Ashfield and back again

The Abbey Craig Trail

Distance **2.3km** Time **45 minutes**
Terrain **formal path, informal forest tracks, some steep sections**
Map **OS Explorer 366** Access **regular bus service from Stirling**

Abbey Craig is an example of a crag and tail hill, formed during the ice age some 12,000 years ago when soft rock (in this case coal) surrounding a harder rock (in this case quartz-dolerite) was worn away by the movement of glaciers through Scotland's Central Belt. Trees cover the whole of the hill and in late spring the woodland floor is carpeted in bluebells.

The Wallace Monument, at the top of the crag, was built in the 1860s following a resurgence in Scottish national identity. It marks the location where, in September 1297, Sir William Wallace had his headquarters prior to the Battle of Stirling Bridge. It was paid for by a public fundraising campaign which included a donation from the Italian nationalist, Giuseppe Garibaldi.

The route begins at the visitor centre at the foot of Abbey Craig. Note that you must pay an entrance fee here if you want to visit the Wallace Monument, but there is no charge to simply walk around the hill. From the visitor centre, follow the footpath as it zigzags up the hill past a series of woodcarvings that represent various stages in Abbey Craig's history.

Briefly join the road that leads up from the car park before turning uphill again,

following the signpost to the Wallace Monument. The monument sits on the summit of Abbey Craig. There are fantastic views across the Central Belt to Ben Lomond, the Arrochar Alps and the Southern Highlands from here.

In the foreground, the loops and bends of the River Forth can be seen; this would surely have been an advantage for Wallace when considering his plans for the battle.

Continue down the hill from the monument, following the blue waymarkers and bearing right to emerge briefly from the trees at a viewpoint across to Stirling Castle and the Gargunnock Hills behind it.

The construction of the Wallace Monument severely damaged the remains of a hillfort that stood on Abbey Craig from around 500AD. Axes and spears have been found on the site, and a turf rampart stands close to this point. The fort was destroyed by fire 100-200 years later but was rebuilt in around 900AD to resist the Vikings.

Carry on down the hill from the viewpoint, keeping straight ahead at a crosspaths and the next junction. Branch

right at the fork beyond this to take a short set of steps down the hill. Bear left at another waymarker to continue down the hill and then left again, following the sign for the visitor centre and car park. From here, the track undulates gently through the woods, climbing gradually back up the hill.

At the top of the hill, turn left, passing an overgrown viewpoint. There is too much foliage to see much, but the summit of Dumyat is visible above the trees. Return to the outward path and head back downhill to the visitor centre.

◀ ● The Wallace Monument on Abbey Craig

Dumyat by the hill path

Distance **8.9km** Time **2 hours 15**
Terrain **well-defined and occasionally
surfaced hill path, rocky in places; vehicle
track and minor country road**
Map **OS Explorer 366 or Harvey's
Superwalker XT25 'Ochil Hills'**
Access **no public transport to the start
of the walk**

**At 418m, Dumyat is not an especially
high hill, but its proximity to Stirling
makes it one of the most popular hills
in the Ochils. The walk is made even
easier by starting halfway up the hill
at the northeastern end of the small
car park on the Sheriffmuir Road, to
the north of Stirling University in
Bridge of Allan.**

From the car park, go through the gate
in the fence and follow the surfaced track
that leads off towards the hill. This route
is very popular and the track was built in
2017 after the original hill path became
badly eroded.

Before long there are excellent views
across Stirling to the Gargunnock Hills.
After climbing a set of stone steps and
rounding the brow of a hillock, the Forth
Valley is laid out before you, looking
down towards Grangemouth Refinery, the
Pentlands and Arthur's Seat in Edinburgh.

The surfaced track soon turns into an
unsurfaced hill track, but the route
towards the top of the hill remains
obvious. It continues through the
foundations of a ruined building. Named

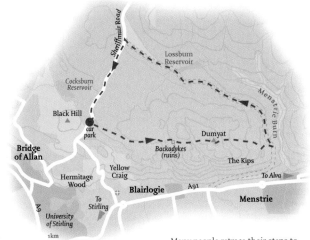

Backadykes, this was a subsistence farmstead run by sub-tenants of nearby Fossachie Farm during the 18th century. It was abandoned in the 1760s as the lands were turned over to sheep.

After 1km or so, the path briefly narrows, with a fairly steep drop on the right, before descending 600m later to pass through a metal gate.

A steeper clamber across rocks is followed by a brief scramble to the summit, where there is a trig point, a beacon and a memorial to the Argyll and Sutherland Highlanders.

The beacon was erected to mark Queen Elizabeth II's Silver Jubilee in 1977. It is traditional to place a stone in it and make a wish. The memorial to the Argyll and Sutherland Highlanders was erected in 2015.

Many people retrace their steps to the car park from here, but for a longer circular walk, continue straight ahead over the summit and follow the track down the eastern slope of Dumyat, bearing left at a fork as you near the bottom of the hill.

Reaching a vehicle track, turn left and follow it for 2km. The track was formerly the Sheriffmuir drove road. This was a popular route with drovers of the 18th and 19th centuries as the slopes of Dumyat represented the last hillside grazing before the cattle market at Falkirk.

Continue straight ahead at a junction to pass the Lossburn Reservoir. Built in 1897, the reservoir is still in operation for the supply of drinking water. Reaching a gateway onto the Sheriffmuir Road, turn left and follow it back to the car park.

◀ Looking up the hill path to the summit

Dumyat by Logie Kirk

Distance **8.9km** Time **3 hours**
Terrain **rough hill track, steep in places**
Map **OS Explorer 366 or Harvey's
Superwalker XT25 'Ochil Hills'**
Access **regular bus service to Blairlogie
from Stirling**

**The Parish of Logie is one of the oldest in
Scotland, dating from the reign of King
David I. Explore ruined churchyards and
dance with the devil on this alternative
route over Dumyat.**

There are several routes to the summit
of Dumyat in addition to the hill path.
This route begins at Blairlogie Meadow
Car Park, just off the A91 to the east of
Blairlogie, and takes a moderately steep
track up the hill's western flank.

Turn left from the top end of the car
park, following the waymarked Hillfoots
Diamond Jubilee Way. Go through the
gate and straight through the hamlet of
Blairlogie. This was the first conservation
area in Central Scotland and still retains
the character of an 18th-century village.

Go through two more gates to cross a
field, following a sign to Logie Kirk. Exit
the field via another gate and follow the
path through the trees, turning right by
Logie Kirk to head up the minor road.

Some 300m along the road you come to
the ruins of Logie Old Kirk. There has
been a church on this site since 1183. The
present ruin dates from around 1684.

Follow the road uphill for 200m beyond
the old kirk before cutting through a gap

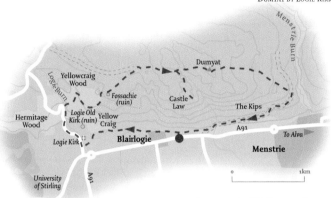

in the wall, fording the Logie Burn and continuing steeply up the tree-covered hill. Climb a set of steps and follow the track through a gap in a fence before continuing uphill again through the trees.

A narrow, almost cave-like passage beneath thick overhanging rhododendron branches leads to a brief, clear plateau. This is Witches Craig. According to legend, it was here that in 1720 the witches of Logie danced with the devil who took the form of a black dog with a blue torch attached to his hindquarters.

Follow the path around to cross a stile and emerge onto the open hillside. A short climb leads to the ruined farmstead of Fossachie. Records of Fossachie date back to the 15th century. In 1692, Major Robert Duncanson of Fossachie was second-in-command of the detachment of Argyle's Regiment at the Massacre of Glencoe. The last tenants were removed in 1761 and the land turned over to sheep.

Continue over the hillside, rounding a corner to meet with the formal grey hill path. After another 600m or so, turn right at a junction with a few small boulders around it to follow an obvious track south towards the two cairns on the summit of Castle Law. The remains of the walls of an Iron Age hillfort can still be seen here. This was the Dun, or 'fort', of the Maeatae, from where Dumyat got its name.

Return to the path and continue to the summit, where there is a trig point, a beacon and a memorial to the Argyll and Sutherland Highlanders.

Head straight over the summit and follow the path down the hill. Nearing the foot, bear right and turn right at the bottom to continue down the hill on a vehicle track.

Approaching a gate, take the waymarked track for the Hillfoots Diamond Jubilee Way, dropping down a set of steps to return to the vehicle track. After 750m, another waymarked track leads back to the car park.

The Darn Road

Distance 4.2km (8.4km return)
Time 1 hour 15 (2 hours 15 return)
Terrain mostly unsurfaced muddy
riverside track **Map** OS Explorer 366 or
Harvey's Superwalker XT25 'Ochil Hills'
Access regular bus and train services to
both Bridge of Allan and Dunblane

Follow in the footsteps of the Romans to discover the inspiration behind a scene in one of Scotland's great literary works.

Local tradition says that the Darn Road was an ancient trackway along the east bank of the Allan Water that was used by the Romans. The name Darn is derived from *dobhran*, the old Gaelic for 'water'. The present Darn Walk, which follows the line of the Darn Road, was developed as a pleasure walk in the late 19th century as Bridge of Allan grew as a spa town and holiday destination.

The walk begins on Blairforkie Drive at the western end of Bridge of Allan. Follow the road along the Allan Water, heading uphill and crossing Allan Walk before taking a narrow track to the left down a set of steps and dropping steeply towards the river again. This old lane was used by horse and cart until 1854.

The path soon opens out to pass a row of trees and the remains of an old mill. There were 10 mills along the Allan between Bridge of Allan and Dunblane at one time, producing items such as corn and meal, flax, wool, cotton, silk, tartan, dyes and paper.

Follow the path along the river, which is home to birdlife such as heron and kingfisher, and through woodland of beech, ash and hazel before descending through an attractive sunken gully into a gorge where Cock's Burn tumbles down into the Allan. Cross the burn by the footbridge, leaving the gully and passing through some beautiful woodland to arrive at a small cave with a pirate-themed carved wooden bench beside it.

This was a favourite location of the 19th-century Scottish author Robert Louis Stevenson. As a sickly child, he had spent

◀ The Darn Road

holidays at the Bridge of Allan Spa, playing along the Darn Road and developing his imagination. This cave is thought to have been the inspiration for Ben Gunn's cave in Stevenson's classic 1883 novel *Treasure Island*. The Darn Road itself features in his 1886 work *Kidnapped*.

Continue along the river, ignoring the concrete footbridge that crosses it, to arrive at Kippenrait Glen, where a bridge crosses the Wharry Burn, a tributary which shortly joins the Allan Water downstream.

These are ancient woodlands. The glen is a designated Site of Special Scientific Interest and a Special Area of Conservation. The Victorian plant collector George Don hooked mosses from the gorge walls with a 15ft pole here to aid his botanical studies. Look out for rare plants such as twayblade and bird's nest orchids. In the spring, the forest floor is carpeted with wild garlic, wood anemone and bluebells. Look out too for the local inhabitants: roe deer, red squirrel, kingfisher, otter and dipper.

Cross the burn and continue up a damp, rock-covered path between two moss-clad drystane dykes. Continuing straight ahead, the path soon opens out to become a pleasant amble along a gentle hillside and the edge of Dunblane Golf Course. Dunblane itself is visible against the southern edge of the Highlands and such distinctive peaks as Ben Ledi, Stùc a'Chroin and Ben Vorlich.

Bear left to leave the golf course by a narrow track, descending gently to a dual-carriageway. Cross over and go down the road directly opposite, heading towards the town centre. Continue straight along the High Street to arrive at Dunblane Cathedral.

Return by retracing your steps, or catch a train back to Bridge of Allan. Alternatively, continue along the Dunblane to Ashfield Riverside Walk, or return to Bridge of Allan by the Glen Road.

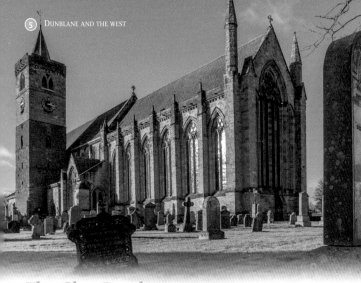

The Glen Road

Distance **5.5km** **Time** **1 hour 30 (one way)**
Terrain **surfaced road or path throughout;**
some mild ascent **Map** **OS Explorer 366 or**
Harvey's Superwalker XT25 'Ochil Hills'
Access **regular bus and train services to**
both Bridge of Allan and Dunblane

The Glen Road slips through Kippenrait
Glen, a steep-sided wooded valley which
carries the Wharry Burn. At one time it
was used by vehicles to get from
Dunblane to Bridge of Allan, but
subsidence caused part of the road to
collapse into the glen in 1987 and it is no
longer safe for vehicles. The collapsed
sections have been secured and the road
has since become a fine surfaced walking
route between the two towns.

Beginning at The Cross in front of
Dunblane Cathedral, and keeping the
cathedral on your left, walk to the end of
the road and follow Sinclairs Street
around St Blane's Church. Turn left onto
the High Street, and follow it to the
Fourways Roundabout, going around it to
the start of Glen Road.

Climb uphill through leafy residential
streets and follow the road out into
gentle, open countryside. Pass the
buildings at Pisgah, an area which takes
its name from the Old Testament
mountain in Moab, east of the Dead Sea.

Beyond a crossroads and a sign
straight ahead for Bridge of Allan, the
road becomes narrow and single track.
At a small car park and three bollards it

◀ Dunblane Cathedral

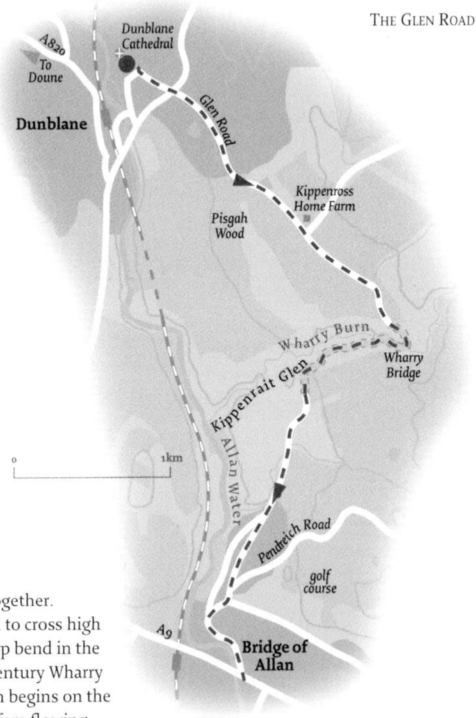

becomes traffic-free altogether.

The route drops down to cross high above the burn at a sharp bend in the road by the early-19th-century Wharry Bridge. The Wharry Burn begins on the slopes of Blairdenon before flowing across Sheriffmuir and through Kippenrait Glen, joining the River Allan a little downstream from here.

The path rises gradually again to lead high along the side of Kippenrait Glen. It is here that the subsidence occurred, and parts of the route are fenced off where the ground has disappeared.

After another three bollards, the path widens to a single-track road and begins to descend into Bridge of Allan, later becoming a wide residential street. Keep right at the fork with Upper Glen Road and, further down, left at the fork with Blairforkie Drive to stay on Glen Road. Turn right at the end of the road, and right again onto Ferniebank Brae. This narrow road soon widens out.

At the bottom, turn left onto Blairforkie Drive and follow it down to the bridge over the Allan and the end of the walk. Retrace your steps to the start of the route, or alternatively, return to Dunblane by the Darn Road, or by train or bus.

17

Blairdenon

Distance **15km** Time **5 hours 15**
Terrain **surfaced roads, hillside tracks,
open moorland** Map **OS Explorer 366 or
Harvey's Superwalker XT25 'Ochil Hills'**
Access **no public transport to the start**

**At 621m, Blairdenon is the most westerly
and perhaps the most remote of the
Ochils' Donalds. The construction of a
new track in early 2015, as part of a
scheme to allow off-road recreational
passage between Menstrie and
Dunblane, has made access much easier
than it has been in the past. This circular
route follows formal and informal tracks,
albeit with a few challenges.**

Beginning in the small car park for Jerah
Woodland, on a corner of the Sheriffmuir
Road, follow the new access road that
crosses the Old Wharry Burn and curves
up the hill. Crossing a shoulder of Big
Hunt Hill, the Forth Valley comes into
view, with Dumyat dominating the west.

Bearing left, the road immediately drops
steeply for a few metres before it begins
to descend more gradually to cross the
Third Inchna Burn. Turn left after 400m
to take a grassy track up the hill beside a
plantation. Cross a wire fence and follow
the track up the slope to meet with an
ATV track. The hill to the northwest is Big
Hunt Hill. Blairdenon is to the northeast.

The ATV track leads across the boggy
plateau of Menstrie Moss to meet with a
fence and a drystane dyke. Double-back to
follow the fence north towards the
imposing mound of Blairdenon. Reaching
a fence by the Old Wharry Burn, climb
over it, clamber down to cross the burn
and begin to ascend, keeping parallel with
the fence and following a vague grassy
track up the hill.

Three fences meet at the unremarkable
summit of Blairdenon. This was the site
of one of the 'Beacons of Dissent', a
protest against the G8 when its leaders

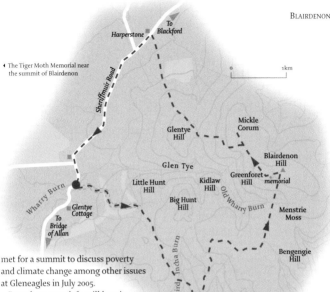

◄ The Tiger Moth Memorial near the summit of Blairdenon

met for a summit to discuss poverty and climate change among other issues at Gleneagles in July 2005.

From here, turn left, still keeping to the fence, to follow another ATV track past the memorial cairn to the pilot of a De Havilland DH82 Tiger Moth which crashed here in August 1957. The memorial is constructed from the remains of the biplane.

Follow the track across Greenforet Hill before swinging right towards Mickle Corum. At a fork, a diversion to the right is worthwhile to reach the cairn at the summit of Mickle Corum, which offers some superb views across the north and west to the Highlands.

Return to the fork and take the other track, which pulls away from the fence and starts to descend. Bear right at the foot of Glentye Hill, and right again a little further on, to pass around the hill.

The ATV track continues straight down the hill. The land to the west of here was used as a training ground during both the First and Second World Wars, and contains the remains of many trenches, gun emplacements and firing ranges.

Reaching the farm at Harperstone, turn left onto the road, following it past the former Sheriffmuir Inn. This 17th-century drovers' inn was once home to Hercules, a huge grizzly bear that had roles in several films, including the 1983 James Bond movie, *Octopussy*. The inn is now a private residence.

Continue along the road back to the start of the walk.

The Battle of Sheriffmuir

Distance 9.1km **Time** 2 hours 30
Terrain well defined and occasionally
surfaced tracks, some quite muddy; some
mild ascent **Map** OS Explorer 366 or
Harvey's Superwalker XT25 'Ochil Hills'
Access regular bus service to Dunblane
from Stirling

The Battle of Sheriffmuir was the
decisive battle of the 1715 Jacobite
Uprising. It pitted 12,000 Jacobite troops
under John Erskine, 6th Earl of Mar,
against 6000 Government troops under
John Campbell, 2nd Duke of Argyll.
The two armies met on Sheriff Muir on
13 November 1715. This walk climbs out
of Dunblane to the edge of the
battlefield, following waymarked trails
named after the opposing commanders,
Argyll and Mar.

Beginning at The Cross, by Dunblane
Cathedral, turn onto Kirk Street and

continue straight ahead up the hill.

By a private car park, take the public
path to Perth Road, walking through the
very pleasant woodland of Holmehill.

Bear left, leaving the woodland, and
then right along Perth Road to cross this
at the zebra crossing. Immediately, turn
up Newton Loan, a narrow lane that runs
beside the grounds of Dunblane Hydro,
eventually becoming a path.

Reaching the end of this, cross the road
and follow Ochiltree, continuing straight
along the path at the end of the road. At
another road, take the path a little to the
right to continue up the hill, turning right
onto the road at the top before climbing
uphill again at Leighton Avenue.

At the first corner, take the rough track
signposted for Sheriffmuir to continue up
the hill. The track becomes increasingly
narrow before reaching a road at Dykedale
Farm. Go straight over the crossroads,

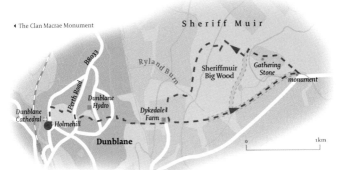

◀ The Clan Macrae Monument

then turn right to follow a surfaced track up the side of a field and into the woodland beyond.

Emerging from the forest, following the Argyll Trail, go straight over two path junctions to arrive at a T-junction. The Clan Macrae Monument, commemorating the Jacobite Clan Macrae's part in the battle, is to your right. At the start of the battle, the Government troops were lined up from here to the Sheriffmuir Inn over to the east.

Follow the signposted Mar Trail to wind your way across the open moorland, crossing a long wooden walkway to reach the Gathering Stone, a collapsed standing stone that has bizzarely been enclosed in an iron cage.

At the beginning of the battle, the Jacobite troops were lined up eastwards from here, parallel to the Government troops. Despite vastly outnumbering the Government troops, Mar was not a leader, and when night fell, both sides withdrew,

each claiming victory. Mar's failure to secure a Jacobite victory contributed to the collapse of the Rising.

The path soon enters the forest again, descending quickly to reach a junction. Turn left, looking out for a narrow, muddy track that leads off down a firebreak on the right. Follow the heather-lined track down to the bottom of the hill. Turn right at a junction by a broken-down old gate and the remains of a steading, bearing left to zigzag down the hill through the trees and meet with a turning circle at the end of a surfaced forest road.

Continue straight ahead along the road, with excellent views across Dunblane through occasional gaps in the trees. Bear right to leave the forest through a gate in the deer fence, crossing the Ryland Burn and walking alongside open farmland.

Turn left along the Argyll Trail again to arrive back at Dykedale Farm, and take the outward path back down to Dunblane.

Dunblane to Ashfield

Distance **7.2km** Time **2 hours**
Terrain **well-defined tracks, surfaced
paths, some short steep slopes**
Map **OS Explorer 366 or Harvey's
Superwalker XT25 'Ochil Hills'**
Access **regular bus service to Dunblane
from Stirling**

**Follow the Allan Water upstream from
Dunblane to the factory village of
Ashfield. The Allan Water rises between
Blackford and Gleneagles and flows
around Strathallan before joining the
River Forth. Watch out for birds such as
dippers, ducks and goosanders. Otters
live on the river too, but they are shy
creatures and you may only see their
tracks. The bolder invasive American
mink is much more likely to be seen.**

The route starts at The Cross, in front
of Dunblane Cathedral. Take the path
towards the river, passing the ruined
Bishop's Palace. Zigzag down the hill,
turning right at the bottom to walk
by the river, passing beneath the
Allan Water Viaduct.

This B-listed railway viaduct was built
for the Scottish Central Railway and was
designed by the Liverpool-based
engineering partnership of Joseph Locke
and John Errington. Begun in 1846 and
opened in 1848 to link Perth and Stirling
to Central Scotland, this railway is still an
important part of the Scottish network.

Pass the elegant 1911 Faery Brig to enter
Laighhills Park. Bear left at the next two
forks to walk around the park, passing a
playpark and swinging around a football
pitch. Hug the riverbank for a little before
bearing right at the next fork, keeping to
the main path. This part of the park is
well-wooded and includes many native
Scottish species.

Climb a steep flight of steps to the top

◀ Looking down the River Allan to Dunblane Cathedral

of Laigh Hill. Keep left at the next fork to head downhill, turning left again to cross a pedestrian bridge over the railway. Continue straight ahead, passing a bridge over the Scouring Burn and bearing left at the next junction, following the signs for Ashfield.

Cross wide-open parkland and brief stretches of woodland before climbing quite steeply to walk along Pont Crescent. Keep left, following the narrow path between the railway line and the houses and descending to meet with the river as it passes beneath the railway. Follow the river beneath the A9 before climbing a short set of steps and continuing north along the edge of an open field.

Where a viaduct carries the railway across the river again, take the underpass beneath the railway, emerging through a gate to continue along the riverbank. Bear left at the next two forks, staying on the riverside until a set of steps climbs uphill, passing a wooden footbridge over the railway to reach Ashfield.

Ashfield is a factory village, built in 1865-66 by J&J Pullar & Co to house workers for their textile printing works, which were powered by the Allan Water. When the factory closed in 1976, it was the last textile printing works in Scotland.

Return to cross the wooden footbridge, turning right at the far end to follow the

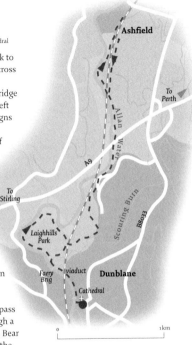

path downhill along the edge of a rough field. Bear left to rejoin the outward route at the underpass.

Follow this path under the A9 and back over the bridge across the railway. Turn left at the far end to follow the path downhill, rejoining the outward route once again at the entrance to Laighhills Park. Follow the river back to the cathedral at the start of the walk.

The villages of Blairlogie, Menstrie, Alva, Tillicoultry, Dollar and Muckhart sit beneath the dramatic southern scarp of the Ochils and are known collectively as The Hillfoots. The 21km-long Hillfoots Diamond Jubilee Way connects the villages, and parts of this route are used by some of the walks in this chapter.

The Way is based on the old King's Highway, the *via regia*. This old road is mentioned in a 14th-century charter by Colin Cambell, Lord of Tullicultry, granting land and oxen to Cambuskenneth Abbey. The highway connected the royal palaces at Stirling and Falkland.

Over the centuries, the Hillfoots villages sprang up where the burns that flow down from the deep, narrow glens – dramatically cleaving the steep southern slopes of the Ochils – intersected with the highway. Today the villages are connected by the A91, which was built as a turnpike road in 1806, replacing the King's Highway, and bypassing the settlements, which simply extended south to encompass the new road.

Perhaps the jewel in the Hillfoots' crown is Castle Campbell, perched dramatically at the top of Dollar Glen, high above the village below.

At the other end of the Hillfoots, Menstrie Castle was home to Sir William Alexander, the 1st Earl of Stirling, founder of Nova Scotia in the early 17th century.

The hills above the Hillfoots are by far the most popular in the Ochils, and many different routes may be accessed from the villages at their feet. The glens at Menstrie, Alva, Tillicoultry and Dollar, as well as Silver Glen between Alva and Tillicoultry, provide five distinct gateways to the hills of the southern Ochils.

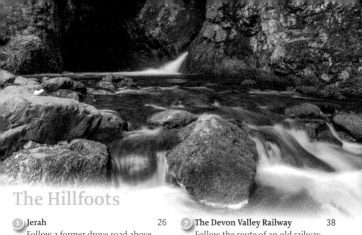

The Hillfoots

1 **Jerah** 26
Follow a former drove road above
Menstrie Glen to reach the crumbling
remains of an old farmhouse

2 **Alva Glen** 28
Ascend this spectacular glen to
discover the mysterious Smuggler's
Cave in the hills beyond

3 **Ben Cleuch by Silver Glen** 30
Look out for hidden riches as you
climb to the Ochils' highest point

4 **Ochil Hills Woodland Park** 32
A fine hillside woodland walk
in the former grounds of Alva House

5 **Mill Glen** 34
Follow the Mill Burn, passing small
waterfalls and crossing several bridges
as you explore this magical glen

6 **Andrew Gannel Hill** 36
A circuit from Tillicoultry to the
summit of this sub-peak of Ben Cleuch

7 **The Devon Valley Railway** 38
Follow the route of an old railway
line which was once hailed as one
of the most beautiful in Scotland

8 **Dollar and Muckhart Mill** 40
Look out for the remains of industry
on the old cart track to Muckhart

9 **Dollar Glen** 42
Climb through Dollar Glen to the
historic castle at its head

10 **King's Seat Hill** 44
Tick off three of the Ochils' Donalds
in this circuit from Dollar Glen

11 **Cadgers' Gate** 46
Beware of ghostly maidens and
dancing fairies in this high pass
between the glens

12 **Hillfoot Hill circular** 48
Circle around Hillfoot Hill to Castle
Campbell, returning by the beautiful
Dollar Glen

Jerah

Distance 9.2km **Time** 3 hours 15
Terrain mostly wide vehicle tracks, some
hillside tracks; some steep climbs
Map OS Explorer 366 or Harvey's
Superwalker XT25 'Ochil Hills'
Access regular bus service to Menstrie
from Stirling

**Follow an ancient drove road to the ruins
of the remote farmstead at Jerah before
crossing the top end of Menstrie Glen
and heading down the lower slopes of
Myreton Hill.**

From opposite the Dumyat Community
Centre, halfway along Menstrie's Main
Street, head up Park Road, turning left at
the far end onto Ochil Road. Just after
crossing the bridge over the Menstrie
Burn, climb the steps on the right,

following a sign for Menstrie Wood.

Go through a gate and climb a steep
path uphill, keeping left at the fork and
quickly leaving Menstrie far below. Pass
the waterworks, continuing along the
steep side of the glen and quickly
climbing to another gate. Turn right onto
a vehicle track that leads around the lower
slopes of Dumyat, which looms above.

This is an old drove road. Dumyat
represented the last hillside pasture
before the drovers reached Falkirk,
and it was a popular overnight stop. After
2km, you arrive at a junction by Lossburn
Reservoir, built in 1897 and still in use.
Turn downhill, keeping right at the next
fork to cross two tributaries of the
Menstrie Burn in quick succession.

Follow the grassy track around the

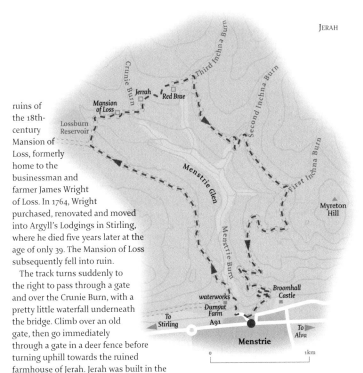

ruins of the 18th-century Mansion of Loss, formerly home to the businessman and farmer James Wright of Loss. In 1764, Wright purchased, renovated and moved into Argyll's Lodgings in Stirling, where he died five years later at the age of only 39. The Mansion of Loss subsequently fell into ruin.

The track turns suddenly to the right to pass through a gate and over the Crunie Burn, with a pretty little waterfall underneath the bridge. Climb over an old gate, then go immediately through a gate in a deer fence before turning uphill towards the ruined farmhouse of Jerah. Jerah was built in the late 18th century. Despite having no running water, it was occupied until the mid-1960s. The name is from the Gaelic *dearg mhagh*, meaning 'Red Plain'.

Follow the grassy track uphill, passing the newly planted Jerah Woodland, eventually joining a wide vehicle track. From here you can see right down Menstrie Glen to distant Alloa and the bridges over the Forth at Kincardine.

Pass the ruins of Red Brae Farmhouse, following the track downhill to cross the Third and Second Inchna Burns. There are

three Inchna Burns in total. The name is from the Gaelic *innis an ath*, meaning 'island of the ford', in reference to an island in the First Inchna Burn

Go through a gate in a deer fence 800m after the Second Inchna Burn, before losing a little height and swinging briefly back into Menstrie Glen. Follow the track as it drops back towards Menstrie, passing Broomhall Castle. Go through a couple of gates before turning right onto Ochil Road and left onto Park Road to return to the start of the walk,

◂ The ruins of Jerah farmhouse

Alva Glen

Distance **3km** Time **1 hour 15**
Terrain **well-maintained though
sometimes steep track to the top of the
glen; hillside tracks with some steep
unfenced drops and some scrambling
required to get down to Smuggler's Cave**
Map **OS Explorer 366 or Harvey's
Superwalker XT25 'Ochil Hills'**
Access **regular bus services to Alva
from Stirling**

This walk follows the scenic Alva Glen to
a waterfall hidden in a cave high in the
Ochil Hills. The Alva Burn tumbles
steeply down from the top of the glen.
By 1830, nine mills were using it to drive
their machinery. A series of dams and
lades were built up its length to regulate
the flow throughout the year.

Look out for the wildflowers that carpet
the forest floor. Kestrels may be spotted
in the cliffs, and long-tailed grey wagtails
can be seen throughout the year. When it
is quiet, roe deer can be seen among the
trees and on the hillside above.

The walk begins at the Alva Glen car
park at the top end of Brook Street in
Alva. Follow the path eastwards to Alva
Glen Quarry. The body of a tiny
prehistoric female was found entombed
here on Christmas Eve 1913 by James
Murdoch, a quarry worker. Bizarrely, two
days later, Murdoch was killed at the
same spot when an overhanging rock
fell on him.

Descend to cross the burn, passing
an impressive waterfall over the Bottom
Dam. Climb the steps, keeping left to
pass beneath an old water pipeline at
the top. Turn immediately left beyond
the pipe to head up the hill and through
a metal gate.

◀ The Alva Burn

The path, dramatically hewn into the cliff face high above the burn, crosses a wooden walkway before levelling with the burn and passing a sign for the Burgh of Alva Water Supply. Another dam is the source of the pipeline that you passed under earlier.

Just before a bridge over the burn, water tumbles down from Lady's Well, a few metres up the cliff. The lady in question is unknown. Perhaps it is Jenny Mutton, a dangerous witch whose spirit is said to haunt Alva Glen. Cross and recross the burn before crossing for a third time at Alva Dam.

A series of switchbacks climb steeply up the hill away from the burn, leading to more and more impressive views down the glen. At the top, the path levels out to arrive at a viewpoint down into Smuggler's Cave. Cross the fence at a stile and follow the track around before bearing right to zigzag downhill, scrambling down some rocks at the bottom to reach the cave.

Here, the roar of the Alva Burn as it flows over a waterfall deep inside the cave is deafening. After visiting the cave, return to the stile and continue uphill, going through a gate and following the fence along the hillside.

This track is known as Pate Road. After a while, the track parts company with the fence, swinging to the right to descend quite steeply towards Alva. The hillside here is terraced. Known as ''The

Delvins' the terraces were used to grow potatoes in the early 19th century.

Follow the track between gorse bushes to go through a gate beside a green of the Alva Golf Course. Climb over a stile at the bottom of the hill, crossing a road to return to the car park.

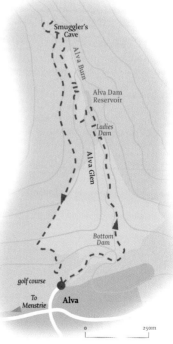

Ben Cleuch by Silver Glen

Distance **11.6km** Time **4 hours**
Terrain **good vehicle track, grassy hill paths, some minor boggy areas and some steep climbs** Map **OS Explorer 366 or Harvey's Superwalker XT25 'Ochil Hills'** Access **regular bus service to Alva from Stirling**

On a clear day, this climb to the highest point in the Ochils is rewarded with a stunning panorama across the whole of the Central Belt. There are several routes up to Ben Cleuch (721m), mostly from the Hillfoot glens. Unsurprisingly, all involve initially steep climbs, but this route, on a vehicle track that leads through Silver Glen, is probably the easiest.

Begin by heading east along the Alva Burn from the Alva Glen car park. Cross the burn by a bridge and climb a series of steps, bearing left to pass beneath a huge waterpipe. Continue straight ahead, turning uphill at the junction and through a gate onto the open hillside.

The hill track leads across the lower slopes of The Nebit to meet with a vehicle track that climbs the hill in a series of switchbacks before straightening out and ascending gently through Silver Glen.

The glen is so called because it contained the richest deposit of silver ore ever found in the British Isles. It was discovered around the time of the 1715 Jacobite Rising. Jacobite landowner

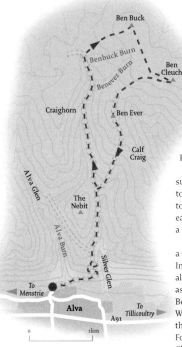

in Ben Lomond and the Cobbler in the west, extending all the way up the Highland Boundary and including Ben Ledi, Ben More, Stob Binnein, Stuc a'Chroin, Ben Vorlich, Ben Lawers and the hills of Perthshire and Angus.

Follow the fence that runs across the summit of Ben Buck, heading southeast towards Ben Cleuch and climbing slowly to cross the fence at a stile. Continue eastwards to the summit, where there is a viewing disc and a trig point.

The view from the summit is surely a contender for the best in Scotland. In addition to the Highland mountains already seen from Ben Buck, you can see as far east as the distinctive pyramid of Berwick Law, Edinburgh, the Pentlands, West Lothian, Tinto Hill and Falkirk. In the immediate foreground, the River Forth snakes from Stirling past the Clackmannan and Kincardine Bridges, the refinery at Grangemouth and the three bridges at Queensferry.

From the summit, a track descends gradually to the southwest before swinging around to follow another fence steeply downhill. Cross the fence at a stile before climbing uphill again to the summit of Ben Ever.

Dropping down on the other side, bear right to cross a brief plateau before descending steeply to meet with the vehicle track again. Turn left and retrace your steps to the start of the walk

Sir John Erskine hid the ore from the government by burying it in the grounds of his home in Alva. After the Rising failed, government specialists, including Sir Isaac Newton, tried to recover the ore, but they found only a few casks full of rocks. The hidden ore had been spirited off to France to fund the Rising.

Follow the vehicle track through the glen, which begins to climb steeply after a ford. Bear right at the fork to follow a grassy track up to the cairn at the summit of Ben Buck. The view from the top takes

Ochil Hills Woodland Park

Distance **3.5km** Time **1 hour 15
Terrain** **well-defined but often steep
forest tracks** Map **OS Explorer 366 or
Harvey's Superwalker XT25 'Ochil Hills'**
Access **regular bus services to Alva
from Stirling**

**What is now the Ochil Hills Woodland
Park was once the grounds of Alva
House. Trees were planted across the
estate and it is believed to be one of the
oldest plantations in Scotland. This
charming walk includes some steep
climbs but is nevertheless a pleasant
woodland ramble along the tree-clad
lower slopes of Wood Hill.**

The route begins in the Ochil Hills
Woodland Park car park, signposted from
the A91 at the eastern end of Alva.

Head out of the car park and take the
path that leads uphill opposite. There are
occasional oak, elm and hawthorn
scattered through this airy sycamore
wood. Bracken and dog's mercury cover
the dark forest floor; in April and May,
there is a spectacular carpet of bluebells.

Look out for birds such as treecreepers,
robins and woodpeckers and if you are
lucky you might even see a buzzard or a
peregrine falcon. Grey squirrels play
among the branches. Shy roe deer may
also be seen in the early morning or
late evening.

At a junction, an interesting short
diversion to the entrance of a silver mine
lies straight ahead, but instead take the
track that climbs steeply uphill. After a
while, the path levels out, becoming a
narrow trail which heads eastwards to
reach a bench at a clearing.

This is a pleasant place to pause and
take in the view: you can see across the
Clackmannanshire countryside towards
the Clackmannan and Kincardine Bridges,
and Grangemouth and Falkirk on the far
side of the Forth.

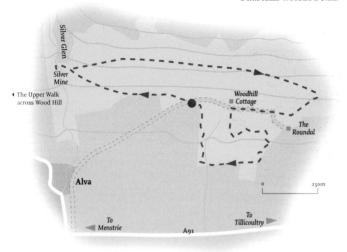

Silver Glen

Silver Mine

◀ The Upper Walk across Wood Hill

Woodhill Cottage

The Roundal

Alva

0   250m

To Menstrie ◀

To Tillicoultry ▶

A91

Continue alongside a moss-covered broken-down stone wall. The path begins to descend gradually. Bear right at a junction, and right again at the bottom of the hill to follow a long straight path which at one time led to Alva House.

Alva House began as a towerhouse in the mid-15th century but was rebuilt as a mansion by the Erskine Family in 1636. It was sold to the Johnstone family in the 1770s and redesigned by the architect Robert Adam in 1789. The last member of the Johnstone family died in the 1920s leaving considerable debts. The house was subsequently used for military target practice during the Second World War. A large, flat rectangular section of ground marks where the house once stood, along with one surviving corner.

Turn right onto a road. Directly opposite a private residence, once Alva House's stables, leave the road, crossing a burn to enter more woodland. This area south of the road was the formal gardens of the house, and shrubs such as rhododendron can be found among the trees. Continue straight ahead, bearing left at the next two junctions.

At the junction after these, continue downhill via some steps, turning left at the bottom and curving round to walk along the foot of the hill. Stay on the main path at the next junction to start heading back uphill again.

Steps lead to a bridge across a burn, before a more substantial set of steps winds further up the hill. Turn left at the top to climb more steps and follow the path back to the car park.

33

Mill Glen

Distance 1.9km **Time** 45 minutes
Terrain well-maintained track to the
top of the glen; occasionally steep
unfenced hillside track to return
Map OS Explorer 366 or Harvey's
Superwalker XT25 'Ochil Hills'
Access regular bus services to Tillicoultry
from Stirling

**Tillicoultry Burn provided a source of
water for the washing and dyeing of wool
in the village's early textile industry,
which in the 18th century was known for
Tillicoultry Serge, a combination of
worsted and linen. The first textile mill,
established in the 1790s, used the burn as
its source of power.**

This route follows the burn up Mill
Glen to the point where it is formed from
the convergence of two smaller burns,
before returning along the steep slopes
of Wester Kirk Craig. Begin by an
ornamental garden at the top of Upper
Mill Street in Tillicoultry. Pass an
information board to head gently uphill
through a gate and immediately into the
dramatic, narrow and high-sided glen.
Tillicoultry Burn tumbles down a series of
waterfalls below the path.

A shallow cave on the right, with water
dribbling down in front of it, is known as
The Lion's Den. The small gully
immediately below the Lion's Den is the
line of the Ochil Fault, where the Earth's
crust split some 300 million years ago to
form the range's steep southern scarp.

Pausing to admire the waterfalls below
from an old stone bridge over the burn,
climb the steps on the other side and
follow the path past the impressive
Craigfoot Quarry at Castle Craig.

Small-scale quarrying was undertaken
at Craigfoot from 1880, but it expanded
greatly when R W Menzies began

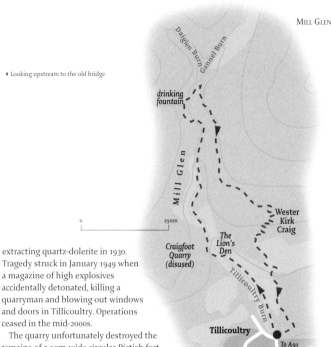

◀ Looking upstream to the old bridge

drinking
fountain

Mill Glen

Daiglen Burn

Gannel Burn

Wester
Kirk
Craig

The
Lion's
Den

Craigfoot
Quarry
(disused)

Tillicoultry Burn

Tillicoultry

To A91

0   250m

extracting quartz-dolerite in 1930. Tragedy struck in January 1949 when a magazine of high explosives accidentally detonated, killing a quarryman and blowing out windows and doors in Tillicoultry. Operations ceased in the mid-2000s.

The quarry unfortunately destroyed the remains of a 90m-wide circular Pictish fort that stood on Castle Craig. According to legend, stone from the fort had been used to build Stirling Castle.

After crossing another three bridges, a long set of wooden steps leads to a fourth bridge. Turn right at the junction beyond the bridge and follow the path past an unusual old drinking fountain which channels water from the waterfall above it. After crossing another bridge the path arrives at the top corner of the glen. The Daiglen and Gannel Burns converge far below to form Tillicoultry Burn. A small barrier here crosses a path which

leads onwards into the hills, but instead swing southwards and continue up a set of stone steps.

Follow the path along the hillside, staying wary of the long drops into the glen below. Bear left at a fork, continuing briefly along the hillside before winding down the hill and heading down a set of steps. Go through a gate and down more steps, turning onto a vehicle track at the bottom and continuing downhill back to the start of the walk.

35

Andrew Gannel Hill

Distance 8.9km **Time** 3 hours
Terrain hillside tracks, initially steep;
wide grassy tracks to the summit; one
short scramble up rocks; avoidable
unfenced track with steep drops on the
return route **Map** OS Explorer 366 or
Harvey's Superwalker XT25 'Ochil Hills'
Access regular bus service to Tillicoultry
from Stirling

This route follows Mill Glen out of
Tillicoultry before climbing The Law
and crossing to Andrew Gannel Hill.
Like a lot of walks from the Hillfoots,
after the initial steep climb – in this case
up The Law – there is an easy canter
around the rolling Ochils plateau.

It has been suggested that the name
of Andrew Gannel Hill, the third highest

hill in the Ochils, is derived from the
Gaelic *An Sruth Gainmheil*, meaning
'sandy-bottomed burn'. But neither the
Andrew Gannel Burn nor the Gannel
Burn, which flow through deep glens on
either side of the hill, are particularly
sandy. More likely is that it was named
after Andrew Gan, who lost his life in a
storm in the 18th century. The name
Andrew Gan Hill dates from at least 1769.

Beginning at the top of Upper Mill
Street in Tillicoultry, follow the path up to
the top corner of Mill Glen (as per the
previous route). Skirt around the barrier
and follow the rocky path down the hill,
crossing the burn at a bridge and climbing
up on the other side.

Here, the path leads almost vertically up
around 2m of rock. After a short scramble,

carry on up the hill. The path climbs quite steeply for a little before levelling out and heading up a wide grassy path which leads to the summit of The Law (638m).

The word *law* is Scots for 'a conical hill', and The Law is distinctly pointed in a range where most of the summits are rounded and featureless. A fence joins the path as you approach the summit, marked by a cairn.

The path levels out beyond the cairn and the Ochils plateau stretches out in front of you, with the glen of the Inner Burn to your left. Across the glen, the summit of Ben Cleuch is not far away.

Approaching the wide saddle that connects Ben Cleuch and Andrew Gannel Hill, bear right to cross a stile and head east along the ridge, dropping briefly to cross the marshy beginnings of the Andrew Gannel Burn before climbing towards the summit (670m). Nearing the flat top, the path swings to the right to arrive at the rocky outcrop of the summit.

Continue eastwards to descend gently from the summit, fording the Gannel Burn and bearing right. At the next fork there is a choice of routes. To the left, the path climbs up and along the wide ridge of a shoulder of King's Seat Hill.

To the right, a narrow path hugs the hillside, leading along the wall of the

steep glen of the Gannel Burn. Until the 1840s this area was known as Gloomingside, and the burn as the Gloomingside Burn, from the Scots *gloaming*. This northwest-facing glen doesn't see much sunlight.

Eventually the two paths converge again, descending gently down Wester Kirk Craig. Soon, you see Craigfoot Quarry gouged into Wood Hill opposite.

Rounding a corner, the path begins to drop. On meeting another path, turn left to zigzag down the hill. At the bottom, turn onto a vehicle track and continue downhill back to the start of the walk.

◀ *Looking towards Tillicoultry from The Law*

The Devon Valley Railway

Distance **7.2km (14.4km return)**
Time **2 hours (4 hours return)**
Terrain **riverside track, level surfaced
path** Map **OS Explorer 366** Access **regular
bus service to Tillicoultry and Dollar
from Stirling; option to return by bus**

**The Devon Way follows an old railway
line that ran between Alloa and Kinross.
The original section of the line, opened in
1851 by the Stirling and Dunfermline
Railway, ran from Alloa to Glenfoot where
engineering difficulties prevented the
crossing of the River Devon. By 1854, the
problems were solved and the line was
opened to Tillicoultry.**

The Devon Valley Railway Company was
formed in 1855 to extend the line to
Kinross, but political issues forced it to be
opened in stages over the next 15 years.
Kinross to Rumbling Bridge opened in
1863, and Tillicoultry to Dollar in 1869. The
final, most difficult section, connecting the
two, opened in 1871. The line was closed
between Dollar and Kinross in 1964 when
passenger services were withdrawn. Coal
was carried from Dollar to Alloa until 1973
when Dollar Mine closed, taking the railway
line with it. This route follows a short
section of the River Devon Trail at
Tillicoultry before joining the old railway
line and heading for Dollar.

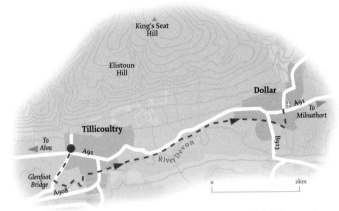

Beginning at the western end of the High Street in Tillicoultry, follow Lower Mill Street out of town. Just before the road crosses the River Devon, turn left through a metal gate to follow the river past the remains of the Devon Viaduct, the cause of the 1851 engineering problems. The huge embankment that had to be built to raise the railway above the river can be seen on the left. The viaduct was dismantled after the line closed.

Continue along the river, passing through a gate and turning left at a crosspaths. After 200m, follow the sign for Dollar to the right to join the route of the old railway line. Stay on the main path to walk along the platform of Tillicoultry Railway Station. The trackbed has been filled in and the station is now a park.

Cross Moss Road at the zebra crossing, the site of a level crossing when the railway was operative. The store to the right of the crossing was formerly Devondale Mill.

Established by J&R Archibald in 1846, the building dates from the 1860s and was a woollen mill, using a waterwheel in the Devon to power its machinery. Production ceased by the First World War, but the building reopened as a paper mill in 1921 and operated until 1972.

From Moss Road, the route leaves Tillicoultry behind and heads out into the countryside to run parallel with the A91. Just beyond a car park on the left is the walled garden of Tait's Tomb, the private burial ground of the Tait family, owners of nearby Harvieston Castle.

Some 750m after passing beneath an old bridge, go straight ahead at a crosspaths, then bear left 300m later to stay on the old railway. Pass beneath two more bridges to reach the derelict platform of Dollar Railway Station. Beyond the station, cross the Dollar Burn and turn left to follow the path down to Bridge Street – the main road that runs through Dollar and the end of the walk.

◀ The Devon Viaduct

Dollar and Muckhart Mill

Distance 11.4km **Time** 3 hours
Terrain mostly good paths, minor country
roads and farm tracks, very muddy in
places; some unmarked tracks through
fields and some mild ascent
Map OS Explorer 366 **Access** regular bus
services to Dollar from Stirling

This picturesque circuit follows the route
of a historic cart track between Dollar and
Muckhart which was the main road
between the two settlements until what is
now the A91 was built in the early 19th
century. The return route passes a
beautiful 17th-century mill.

Beginning opposite the memorial clock
by the bridge over the Dollar Burn, follow
Park Place along the side of the burn to its
southern end. Continue straight ahead
past the primary school, turning left at the
far end and following the route of the old

railway line to reach Gowan Lea. A dirt track
leads off behind some houses. This is the
beginning of the old road to Muckhart.

Follow the track eastwards, turning
uphill at Westerton Farm Cottage before
continuing eastwards again. Where there
are two gates side by side, go through the
one on the left.

Reaching a road, go right to continue
eastwards, turning off after 100m to follow
the signposted Old Road to Vicar's Bridge.
This is one of the last surviving sections of
the old cart track – parts of it have been
worn so much that they are significantly
lower than the surrounding land.

After crossing a little wooden bridge,
the path exits onto a wide field. Turn
uphill, following the edge of the field to a
gate at the top. Turn left onto the road,
going straight ahead at the crossroads
along the signposted old road to Muckhart.

◀ Muckhart Mill

The road drops to cross the Hole Burn at a bridge by a ford before continuing uphill along another well-worn old track.

Pass around the trees and walk through a couple of gates and then Leys Farm. At a road, turn right, passing Muckhart Primary School, going right again after 300m to leave the road and bear south over the hill.

Reaching a T-junction, turn right again. The great cleft of Dollar Glen rips into the hillside straight ahead.

Swing downhill past the remains of a 19th-century limekiln. This was operated by the Carron Company and manufactured lime for use in their ironworks at Camelon near Falkirk.

Muckhart Mill is immediately ahead, sitting on the confluence of the Hole Burn and the River Devon. This beautiful old corn and flour mill still has the waterwheel on the side, although it is no longer operational. Originally named Blairbane, it is now a private residence. Records of the mill go back to 1560, though the present building dates from 1666.

Cross the old bridge over the Hole Burn, which powered the mill, and continue straight ahead to return to the crossroads. Turn left and follow the road, going right at a junction. Pass the entrance to the Old Road to Vicar's Bridge and retrace your steps to Dollar.

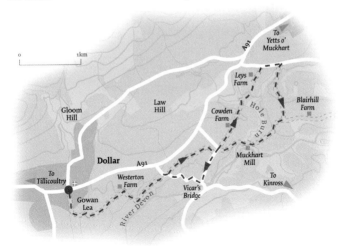

Dollar Glen

Distance 3.2km **Time** 1 hour 45
Terrain hillside tracks, some steep; there
are also steep unfenced drops
Map OS Explorer 366 or Harvey's
Superwalker XT25 'Ochil Hills'
Access regular bus service to Dollar
from Stirling

Climb a narrow wooded glen to a castle
perched high on the hillside above Dollar.
Castle Campbell was known as Castle
Gloom, from the Gaelic *glom* for 'chasm',
when built around 1430. It sits between
the romantically named Burns of Care and
Sorrow, which converge to form the Dollar
Burn near the bottom of the glen. This
circular route follows the Dollar Burn and
then the Burn of Care up to the castle,
before returning along the Burn of Sorrow.

The walk begins at the top end of East
Burnside in Dollar, where a path through
a gap in the wall is signposted to Castle
Campbell. Cross Mill Green, named after
the medieval meal mill that once stood
here, and follow the Dollar Burn past a
stone viewing platform and up into the
narrow glen.

Over to your left, as you continue along
a walkway, the Burn of Sorrow flows
through the narrow canyon of Windy Edge
Pass to converge with the Burn of Care.
The walkway follows the Burn of Care past
Hempy's Falls and across a footbridge.
Castle Campbell is now high on the hill
directly above.

Immediately ahead, the burn plunges
down the impressive Craiginnan Falls, but
the path itself snakes up the hill to the
castle entrance. Between the 15th and 19th
centuries, Castle Campbell was the

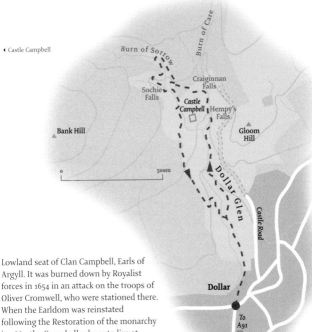

◀ Castle Campbell

Lowland seat of Clan Campbell, Earls of Argyll. It was burned down by Royalist forces in 1654 in an attack on the troops of Oliver Cromwell, who were stationed there. When the Earldom was reinstated following the Restoration of the monarchy in 1661, the Campbells chose to live at Argyll's Lodging in Stirling, though they continued to own the castle. Today, the castle is run by Historic Scotland and is worth a visit if open.

Turn away from the castle and (ignoring the path that drops down to the burn), continue left past a bench and up the hill. At a fork, a brief detour to the left leads to the beautiful Sochie Falls. Returning to the fork, head up the hill and through a gate to follow the Burn of Sorrow past more waterfalls, crossing it by a footbridge. Turn left at the junction to zigzag down a steep

path and cross another footbridge. Bear right to cross the burn again and pass a gate where a short diversion leads down to the Windy Edge Pass Viewpoint; here, the Burn of Sorrow disappears through the narrow ravine to join the Burn of Care.

Back at the gate, the path rises to a bench with a viewpoint across to the castle before dropping back down into the glen. Cross the burn and turn right to cross Mill Green and return to the start of the walk.

King's Seat Hill

Distance **12.1km** Time **4 hours 15**
Terrain **well-defined but often steep hill
tracks** Map **OS Explorer 366 or Harvey's
Superwalker XT25 'Ochil Hills'**
Access **regular bus service to Dollar
from Stirling**

**This high-level circuit climbs to the
summit of King's Seat, a peak tinged with
tragedy. The route also takes in Bank,
Tarmangie, Whitewisp and Saddle Hills.**

According to legend, at some point in the
latter half of the 11th century, a hunt was
organised for a huge and vicious boar that
was making a nuisance of itself around the
local villages. King Malcolm Canmore
himself was in attendance, choosing to
observe proceedings from the hill that was
thereafter known as King's Seat.

From the top end of East Burnside in
Dollar, follow the Dollar Burn up to Castle
Campbell (as per the previous route). Take
the path just outside the castle gateway,
dropping down to cross a bridge over the
Burn of Sorrow, and continue up the hill on
the other side.

At the top, cross the stile and follow the
path by the fence, bearing left at the next
two forks to climb to the cairn at the top
of Bank Hill. Follow the track around the
cairn, which leads through a gate in an old
drystane dyke, and on up King's Seat Hill.

Around 12 noon on 16 January 1943, three
Spitfires from RAF Grangemouth crashed
into the southern face of the hill. Two of
the pilots were killed. Despite sustaining

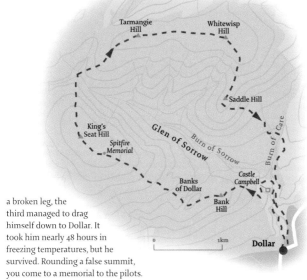

a broken leg, the third managed to drag himself down to Dollar. It took him nearly 48 hours in freezing temperatures, but he survived. Rounding a false summit, you come to a memorial to the pilots.

The view from the large cairn at the top of the hill is incredible, taking in Loch Leven, the Lomond Hills and the Forth Valley. Strike out northwest from the cairn, bearing right at a small cairn which marks the true summit. Drop steeply down to cross the Burn of Sorrow at a secluded spot where two of its tributaries meet before tumbling through the Glen of Sorrow towards Castle Campbell.

The climb out of the Glen of Sorrow is steep, levelling a little before meeting the corner of a drystane dyke. Follow the dyke to the summit of Tarmangie Hill, crossing a stile to reach its two cairns and returning through a gate to the south side of the dyke. Follow this eastwards to the small cairn at the summit of Whitewisp Hill.

From here, turn right to descend towards Saddle Hill, keeping right to reach the small plateau and the cairn at its summit. Castle Campbell can be seen at the head of Dollar Glen. There are no distinct paths off Saddle Hill. Turn southeasterly from the cairn, aiming for a shallow gully that runs diagonally down the side of the hill. A path leads down the gully to the base of the hill.

Follow the path down towards an old sheep pen at Craiginnan, passing through it and continuing straight ahead, veering left to join a vehicle track. Ford the Burn of Care twice before going through a gate, following the track downhill through another gate and then a third gate by a cottage. Follow the road back downhill into Dollar.

◀ The Spitfire Memorial on King's Seat Hill

Cadgers' Gate

Distance **7.8km** Time **2 hours (4 hours return)** Terrain **good but occasionally muddy or steep track** Map **OS Explorer 366 or Harvey's Superwalker XT25 'Ochil Hills'** Access **regular bus service to Dollar from Stirling; no public transport to Glendevon**

Cadgers' Gate is the southernmost section of the old drove road, known as the Cadgers' Way, which ran between Dollar and Auchterarder. This walk follows the Way as it climbs from Dollar through a mysterious narrow pass to traverse the entire length of Glen Quey.

It has been suggested that Glen Quey got its name from the Scots *kye*, meaning 'cattle', which fits with the drove road that runs through it. But it might also be derived from the Gaelic *Gleann Coimhich*, the 'stranger's' or 'foreigner's glen', in recognition not only of the drovers, but also of the tinkers, or cadgers, who used the route.

From Dollar, follow Dollar Glen as far as Castle Campbell (as per the previous two routes). The access road at the front of the castle loops around to the right to ford the Burn of Care. At a cottage by a gate, double back on yourself, following the sign for Cadgers' Gate. Stick to the main path to climb away from Dollar Glen and into the Glen of Care.

Take the middle path at a three-way fork, still climbing to eventually level out as the glen narrows into a slender pass between Whitewisp and Hillfoot Hills.

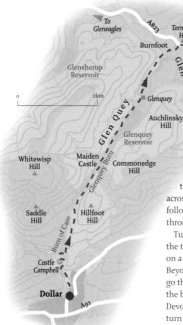

in the outside world.

Rounding Maiden Castle, the pass suddenly opens out into Glen Quey, with the eponymous reservoir stretching out ahead. Descend into the glen to walk along the shore. Passing the dam at the far end, go through a gate and across a stile, turning immediately left to follow a grassy track northeastwards and through a gate in a deer fence.

Turn downhill at a crosspaths, following the track signed for Glendevon to emerge on a road at the hamlet of Burnfoot. Beyond a bridge over the Glenquey Burn, go through the gate on the left to follow the burn to its confluence with the River Devon. Cross the Devon at the footbridge, turn right at the main road and follow it to the Tormaukin Hotel and the walk's end.

The Tormaukin began as a natural stopping place for 18th-century drovers taking their cattle through Glen Devon or over the Cadgers' Way to the ferry at Alloa and onwards to the market at Falkirk. The historic inn is one of the best known in Scotland and counts Neil Armstrong, Charlie Chaplin, and Laurel and Hardy among its former guests.

Return to Dollar by the same route. Alternatively, make a circular route by climbing Innerdownie, or – for the more adventurous – continue onwards to Auchterarder via Cadgers' Yett and Cloan Glen.

Beyond a large boulder in the middle of the track, a small pool sits between the path and the burn. This is Maiden's Well. According to local folklore, the spirit of a young woman who inhabits the pool appears at night, but any attempt to kiss her will result in certain death.

Beyond Maiden's Well, the track circumvents a large hillock named Maiden Castle. Despite its name, there has never been a castle here but, according to legend, the hill contains a fairy castle. One night, a piper on his way to Castle Campbell was invited in to play for the fairies. When he left, 100 years had passed

◂ Glen Quey from Maiden Castle

Hillfoot Hill circular

Distance 6.5km **Time** 2 hours 15
Terrain wide, sometimes steep vehicle
track, hillside tracks **Map** OS Explorer 366
or Harvey's Superwalker XT25 'Ochil Hills'
Access regular bus service to Dollar from
Stirling. Walk to start point via Dollar
Glen, or alternatively start and end at
Castle Campbell

Much of the commercial forestry around
Hillfoot Hill, by Dollar, has been felled,
leaving clear views across Fife and Kinross.
This route circles the hill's tree-covered
summit before heading down to Castle
Campbell and returning by Dollar Glen.

To get to the start point, follow Upper
Hillfoot Road out of Dollar. The walk
begins in the Lawhill Community
Woodland car park on the right, around
370m beyond Tarmangie Drive.

Turn right out of the car park and follow
the road for a short distance, before
turning uphill through a set of gates and
onto a tree-lined driveway. Bear right to go
through another gate, quickly leaving the
trees behind. Soon the road turns back on
itself in a tight hairpin bend to become a
rough vehicle track. This climbs fairly
steeply, with views opening out over to
Loch Leven and the Lomond Hills.

Where the main track bends uphill in
another hairpin, continue along the
smaller track that leads off straight ahead.
This plantation has been cleared and is
being redeveloped as Dollar Forest,
including improvements to paths and
cycle tracks.

The track continues around the hill
before descending southeast in a long
straight stretch, with views down Dollar
Glen to the Forth, and the huge bulk of
Whitewisp and Saddle Hills to the right.

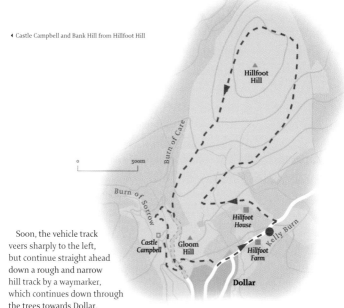

◄ Castle Campbell and Bank Hill from Hillfoot Hill

Soon, the vehicle track veers sharply to the left, but continue straight ahead down a rough and narrow hill track by a waymarker, which continues down through the trees towards Dollar.

Bear left at the junction to continue downhill on a more formal path. Rounding a corner and going through a gate, you see Castle Campbell standing guard at the top end of Dollar Glen below you. The castle, high on the hillside above Dollar, is one of the most dramatically positioned in Scotland. This path offers one of the best vantage points, looking down on the castle with the view uninterrupted by trees and foliage.

Turn right by a cottage to cross the Burn of Care. At the castle entrance, take the steps to the left down into Dollar Glen.

Beyond a footbridge, bear left and left again, climbing uphill to the car park on Castle Road.

Turn uphill, shortly taking the path on the right that leads off through the trees past the overgrown, disused Gloomhill Quarry, where a quartz-dolerite sill was worked for road stone.

Continue along the path, which joins a fence along the edge of the woodland above Dollar. Drop down to join Upper Hillfoots Road at the end of the fence, turning left to return to the start of the walk.

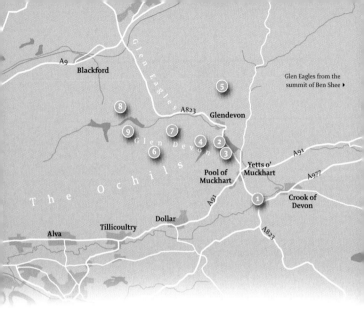

Glen Eagles from the summit of Ben Shee ▶

The River Devon begins high in the Ochils before running eastwards, then southeast through Glen Devon. The glen is joined from the north by Glen Eagles.

The River Devon has been dammed in three places, creating substantial reservoirs at Castlehill and the Upper and Lower Glendevon Reservoirs. Two further reservoirs have been created by damming tributaries in Glen Quey and Glen Sherup. Between them, these provide a water supply to Dunfermline and West Fife.

This route across the Ochils has been used for centuries. A drove road, used by drovers taking their cattle between the markets at Crieff and Falkirk, ran through the glen on the opposite side to the modern road. As such, a gateway (or Yett) at Muckhart, where tolls were collected from the drovers at a rate of one shilling a score, was established at Muckhart in the early 19th century.

A 14km Reservoirs Trail, created by the Woodland Trust, links Muckhart to the Upper Glendevon Reservoir via the other four reservoirs, utilising parts of the old drove road. Several sections of the Trail, along with other parts of the drove road, are used by the walks in this chapter.

The A823 runs through Glen Devon and then Glen Eagles. Taking advantage of this low pass, it links Muckhart in the south with Auchterarder in the north. The road offers easy access to the hills in the heart of the Ochils with the access roads to the reservoirs providing further ingress.

Glen Devon and Glen Eagles

1 **Rumbling Bridge Gorge** 52
Beginning as a picturesque gorge walk, this circular woodland route follows the Devon to Crook of Devon

2 **Castlehill Upper Loop** 54
A stunning hillside walk on the slopes above Castlehill Reservoir

3 **Seamab Hill** 56
Climb the three hills that stand guard over the southern entrance to Glen Devon

4 **Innerdownie** 58
A straightforward climb to the summit of the smallest of the Ochils' Donalds, returning by Glenquey Reservoir

5 **Cadgers' Yett** 60
This traditional route through the hills was used by travelling folk in times past

6 **The Glen Sherup Horseshoe** 62
Bag three of the Ochils' Donalds in one go in this popular circuit

7 **Ben Shee** 64
Get away with the fairies in this circular route with splendid views along Glen Devon

8 **Wether Hill** 66
Climb to the summit of Wether Hill, which stands sentinel above Glen Eagles, returning along the old drove road

9 **The Frandy Reservoirs** 68
An easy walk past two of the Ochils' great reservoirs

Rumbling Bridge Gorge

Distance 5.8km **Time** 1 hour 30
Terrain good forest and riverside paths;
a small section on a roadside pavement
Map OS Explorer 369 **Access** bus service
from Stirling to Rumbling Bridge

**This walk leads from the stunning
Rumbling Bridge Gorge along the River
Devon to the nearby village of Crook of
Devon, returning via an attractive
woodland path.**

The route begins in a lay-by off the
A823, to the north of the village of
Rumbling Bridge, where a fascinating
double bridge carries the road 37m above
the River Devon. It gets its name from
the rumbling noise caused by boulders
grinding in the waterfalls below. The
lower bridge, 26m above the water,
was built in 1713 by William Gray of
Saline. The road above was levelled and a
new bridge built on top of the original

bridge in 1815-16 by road engineer
Charles Abercrombie.

A woodland path, signposted for Crook
of Devon, leads off through the trees at
the southern end of the lay-by. Looking
back, you can see the bridge sitting high
over the River Devon, though there are
better views of it on the return journey.

Between the late 1930s and early 1970s,
a collection of Roman coins was found
buried in these woods. The hoard is now
in the possession of the National
Museum of Scotland in Edinburgh.

Continue along the path, dropping
down a set of wooden steps and passing
a stone seating area to leave the gorge and
walk along the riverbank. The large tree-
covered mound to the south, known as
Spinneyburn, is believed to be a
prehistoric burial site.

Further on, a weir across the river is part
of the Rumbling Bridge Community

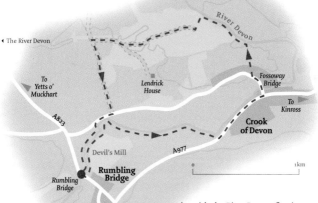

◀ The River Devon

Hydro Scheme – the largest community owned hydroelectric project in Britain.

Water flows from this weir down a 1.4km pipeline that has been buried in an old railway cutting, dropping a total of 41m to two 250kW turbines housed in an underground powerhouse south of Rumbling Bridge. With water flowing in excess of 2.3 cubic metres per second, the scheme has been producing a steady 500kW of renewable energy since 2016.

At the top of a long flight of steps, turn left and walk along the pavement into Crook of Devon. Reaching Naemoor Road, follow the sign back towards Rumbling Bridge, crossing the 18th-century Fossoway Bridge over the Devon. Look out for a narrow path on the right that leads back to Rumbling Bridge.

The path drops steeply to meet, once

again, with the River Devon, flowing eastwards this time. From here, the river doubles tightly back on itself like a shepherd's crook, giving the village its name. Do not cross the bridge that is straight ahead, but instead continue along the riverbank, passing through a gate and following another signpost for Rumbling Bridge onto a wide forest path between Scots pines and other conifers. Ignore the path that leads off to Lendrick House. Beyond a gate, turn left onto a narrow country road and follow it back towards Rumbling Bridge.

Reaching a junction, follow the road to the right for 160m before turning into the woodland to walk along the riverbank and back into Rumbling Bridge Gorge. There are various options to leave the path to view the river as it tumbles over a series of spectacular waterfalls and forces its way through narrow stone passages.

Eventually the path climbs a set of steps and returns to the start of the walk.

Castlehill Upper Loop

Distance **4.4km** Time **1 hour 15**
Terrain **good waymarked hillside paths,
boggy in places; some mild ascent**
Map **OS Explorer 366 or Harvey's
Superwalker XT25 'Ochil Hills'**
Access **no public transport to the start**

**Enjoy a pleasant ramble through native
Scottish woodland in this hillside walk.
The Woodland Trust has planted more
than 1.5 million trees along Glen Devon
since it acquired the land back in 2000,
as part of a project to regenerate the area
and restore it to the native woods that
would have existed here centuries ago.**

The restored woodland is home to roe
deer, fox, hedgehog, red squirrel, pine
marten and bats, while short-eared owls
and kestrel may also be spotted around
here. This route, through an area known
as Geordie's Wood, is one of several

walking trails up and down the glen
that have been created by the Trust.
Cross the road from the southern end
of the lay-by halfway up Castlehill
Reservoir, just off the A823. Head up the
single-track private road signposted for
Glenquey Reservoir. There are two
waymarked walks on the hillside above
the reservoir – red for the shorter Lower
Loop and green for the longer Upper
Loop that this route follows.

After 300m go through a gate on
the left into the Glendevon Woodlands,
following the track across a couple of
bridges and swinging around to walk
uphill alongside an old drystane dyke.
Turn left at the junction, descending
slightly before taking a track that leads
off up the hill again.

The path climbs to another junction,
facing the thick wall of the conifer

◀ The view towards Seamab Hill from Castlehill Upper Loop

plantation that crowns Auchlinsky Hill, and veers sharply right to continue uphill, now bearing north. Oak, ash, birch, hazel, rowan, juniper and Scots pine are among the species that you'll find here on what was previously grazing land for sheep.

Further on, as you start to head west, you come to a viewpoint by a gap in a broken-down drystane dyke. Ben Thrush is straight ahead, with the turbines of the Green Knowes Windfarm on the horizon. Next to that, White Creich Hill and Tormaukin sit a little to the east, while Down Hill can be seen directly across the Castlehill Reservoir.

The path becomes wider from here. Meeting a vehicle track, continue downhill to reach a gate in a deer fence. Turn right onto the single-track road beyond the gate. Follow it past a cottage and back down to the start of the walk.

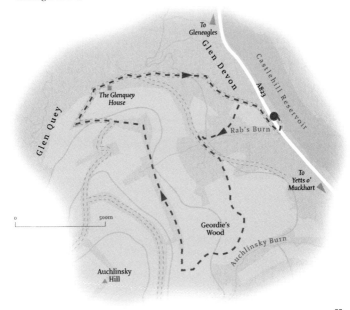

Seamab Hill

Distance **10.4km** Time **3 hours 30**
Terrain **forest vehicle tracks, hillside tracks, some moderately steep**
Maps **OS Explorer 366 and 369 or Harvey's Superwalker XT25 'Ochil Hills'**
Access **no public transport to the start**

Standing guard over the southern end of Glen Devon, Seamab Hill may not be as tall as some of the other peaks in the Ochils, but it is one of the more prominent. This route climbs through the timber plantation on Auchlinsky Hill before crossing the summit of Commonedge Hill and finishing on Seamab Hill.

Beginning at the southern end of the lay-by halfway up Castlehill Reservoir, cross the A823 and follow the private road towards Glenquey Reservoir for 1.2km.

Just past a cottage, at a gate signed for Geordie's Wood, follow a vehicle track uphill. Geordie's Wood has been recently planted by the Woodland Trust. The timber plantations that formerly covered the area have been replaced with native trees such as oak, ash, birch, hazel, rowan and Scots pine.

Passing through a second gate, the track enters the huge commercial forestry plantation which still clads most of the summit of Auchlinsky Hill. Bear left to follow the broad but rough track which gently circles the summit, occasionally catching a glimpse of Castlehill Reservoir through the trees, before veering sharply uphill to cross the shoulder of the hill, hidden beneath the trees. Innerdownie Hill lies straight ahead.

Turn left, rejoining the vehicle track you left earlier and following it out of the trees and onto the exposed grassy plain of

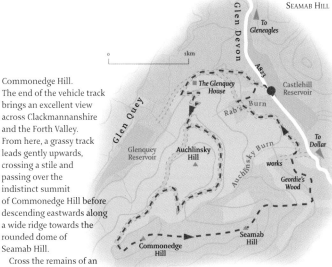

Commonedge Hill.
The end of the vehicle track brings an excellent view across Clackmannanshire and the Forth Valley. From here, a grassy track leads gently upwards, crossing a stile and passing over the indistinct summit of Commonedge Hill before descending eastwards along a wide ridge towards the rounded dome of Seamab Hill.

Cross the remains of an old drystane dyke and a stile in a deer fence, and up the final incline to the summit of Seamab Hill, marked by a small cairn. This is a fine viewpoint, looking north across Castlehill Reservoir and taking in the Lomond Hills, Loch Leven, North Berwick Law, Knock Hill (with the communication masts on its summit) and the Pentlands.

Continue straight across the summit to drop steeply downhill and go through a gateway in a broken-down drystane dyke. Carry straight on, passing through another drystane dyke before following it down the hill past a bench and across a crossroads of paths.

At the bottom of the hill, pass through a gate and bear left along a narrow track between two fences, following the Reservoirs Trail. A gate in a deer fence leads back into the young Geordie's Wood. The native trees that have been planted here encourage birdlife such as kestrel and short-eared owls.

Reaching the access road for the water treatment works, cross over and continue down the track opposite. Cross the Auchlinsky Burn at a small bridge and go through a gate, swinging left to cross the fence again at a stile, signposted as an 'Old Drover's Road'. Follow the fence northwards, eventually leaving it behind as the track widens.

When you come to a waymarker, turn downhill past a picnic bench, passing through another gate in the deer fence and joining the private road of the outward route. Continue downhill back to the start.

Innerdownie

Distance **8.4km** Time **3 hours**
Terrain **good if sometimes steep hillside paths, brief vehicle track**
Map **OS Explorer 366 or Harvey's Superwalker XT25 'Ochil Hills'**
Access **no public transport to the start**

At 611m, Innerdownie is the smallest of the Ochils' Donalds, just scraping into the classification. The name of the hill is derived from the Gaelic *Inbhir*, meaning 'confluence', and *Dùnaigh*, 'hillfort', probably in reference to the fort on nearby Down Hill. This is an easy romp up the eastern slope before descending to return via Glen Quey.

Start at The Tormaukin Hotel in Glendevon village. If you intend to dine at The Tormaukin, you may park in the front car park at the landlord's discretion. Cross the road and turn left, continuing to the end of the path and crossing back again to follow the signposted 'Path to Dollar' over a bridge across the River Devon. Follow the grassy track to a road, turning to cross the Burnfoot Bridge over Glenquey Burn.

Passing a house, a track sets out uphill past a sign for Glendevon Woodlands. Go through a gate in a deer fence, continuing up the hill and over a staggered crosspaths. The steep, grassy path soon passes a bench, with views across Glendevon village and Linn Hill next to it. Castlehill Reservoir stretches out beyond to the southern end of the glen. This shoulder of Innerdownie is Glenquey Hill, named after the glen on its southern side.

Beyond the bench, the gradient eases. Reaching a waymark post, the wide grassy ridge of Innerdownie opens out ahead.

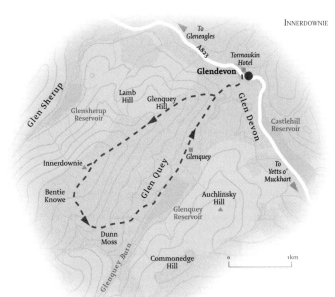

On the map:
To Gleneagles
A823
Tormaukin Hotel
Glendevon
Glen Sherup
Lamb Hill
Glensherup Reservoir
Glenquey Hill
Glen Devon
Castlehill Reservoir
Innerdownie
Glen Quey
Glenquey
To Yetts o' Muckhart
Bentie Knowe
Auchlinsky Hill
Glenquey Reservoir
Dunn Moss
Glenquey Burn
Commonedge Hill
0   1km

Soon, the track meets with a drystane dyke, which it follows all the way to the rounded knob of the summit straight ahead.

Bear right at the fork just before the final short steep pull to the summit, which is marked by a cairn. From here the Highland Boundary can be clearly seen, with Stùc a'Chroin and Ben Vorlich prominent on the northern horizon, as well as the distant pyramid of Schiehallion.

Return to the fork and take the other path to pass beneath the summit, bearing right and swinging downhill across an area known as Dunn Moss. At the bottom of the hill, ford the Dunnmoss Burn to walk along the northern shore of Glenquey Reservoir, eventually continuing along a vehicle track. The reservoir was

built by the Dunfermline Corporation Water Works and was opened in 1909.

Beyond the dam, go through a gate, then a few metres later cross a stile. Look out for an old bee-bole, used to shelter beehives, built into the drystane dyke. Beyond the stile, turn immediately left through another gate to leave the vehicle track. Follow the path northeastwards, passing through a gate in a deer fence and into Glenquey Woodland.

This land was used for sheep grazing for 250 years, before being acquired by the Woodland Trust in 2000. By 2008, around 1.5 million native trees had been planted. Continue along the path to reach the staggered crosspaths of the outward route. Turn right and retrace your steps to Glendevon village.

◄ The view from the summit shelter

Cadgers' Yett

Distance **14.1km** Time **4 hours 45**
Terrain **muddy hill track, hillside ATV
tracks, surfaced roads; some steep climbs**
Map **OS Explorer 366 or Harvey's
Superwalker XT25 'Ochil Hills'**
Access **no public transport to the start**

The turbines of the Green Knowes
Windfarm are your constant companion
on this route along Cadgers' Yett, the
middle section of the old drove road
between Dollar and Auchterarder. A
cadger, or tinker, was an itinerant trader
who would travel from town to town
selling wares or services. Though now
used as a derogatory term, tinkers were
often relied upon and were highly
regarded members of society.

Start at The Tormaukin Hotel in
Glendevon village. If you intend to dine at
The Tormaukin, you may park in the front
car park at the landlord's discretion. From
the car park, turn left to leave the village.
At a sign for the path to Auchterarder,
take the track uphill, passing through the
gates of Glenfoot House. Further on, go
through the left of two gates and follow
the track into Borland Glen.

Ben Thrush rises steeply above, topped
with the huge turbines of the windfarm
which was completed in 2008. The route
has been quite enclosed up to now, but at
a broken-down gate at the highest point
of the pass, the view opens out across
Auchterarder and Strathearn to Crieff and
the Southern Highlands.

Look out for the sparse remains of an old farmstead as you descend along the Hodyclach Burn. Cross the burn by an old bridge and go through a couple of gates. A final wooden gate leads to a surfaced road at Coulshill.

Continue along the road, turning across a cattle grid towards Bankfold Farm and climbing between two gates side by side. Go through the gate on the right and follow an obvious ATV track, which runs parallel to a fence for a little before passing through another gate by a copse of trees.

Continue straight up the hill towards the trig point at the top of Steele's Knowe. Cross the summit towards the nearest of the wind turbines, which stretch into the distance across the hillside alongside a service road. Each turbine is numbered – this is number 5. Bear left to walk along the road, taking the road signed for the exit beyond turbine 11.

Looking southwest from here, you can see Glen Sherup, with Innerdownie and Tarmangie on its left and Scad Hill and Ben Shee on its right. Behind them, Andrew Gannel Hill, Ben Cleuch, Ben Buck and the turbines of the Burnfoot Hill Wind Farm line the horizon.

Bear left to head for turbine 17 and Ben Thrush. The road ends beyond turbine 18 but an ATV track leads on, forking right after 20m towards the cairn on the summit of Ben Thrush.

The view from here is superb, taking in Glen Devon as it stretches southeast past the distinctive peak of Down Hill and the Castlehill Reservoir, and west towards Common Hill and Glen Eagles. Glendevon village is immediately below you.

Return to the fork by the turbines and follow the other track around the left of the summit, cutting back down towards Glen Devon to reach a gate in a drystane dyke. Go straight across the field, going through the gate on the left at the far side, and doubling immediately back through another gate to follow the outward route back to Glendevon.

◀ Heading down into Glen Devon from Ben Thrush

The Glen Sherup Horseshoe

Distance **15.8km** Time **5 hours 30**
Terrain **vehicle tracks, good hillside
tracks; steep climbs** Map **OS Explorer 366
or Harvey's Superwalker XT25 'Ochil Hills'**
Access **no public transport to the start**

This classic route follows the southern
side of Glen Sherup, traversing the hills
of Innerdownie, Whitewisp and
Tarmangie, before crossing the head of
the glen and returning along the north
side over Scad Hill and Ben Shee.

Beginning at the Glen Sherup car park,
follow the path for the Ben Shee Loop to
merge onto the wide forest access road,
swinging left and ascending gently
around Black Hill, bearing left to pass a
small open-cast quarry and weave around
Gled's Nose and Lamb Hill.

By a cairn, take the path that leads
steeply up the hill along a firebreak
carpeted in pine-needles, emerging from
the trees through a gate and coming
suddenly upon a sweeping view of the
hills on the far side of Glen Devon.

Follow the path uphill, bearing right
below the summit of Innerdownie to
make the short but steep climb to the
cairn. Just beyond the summit, a ruined
shelter is built into a drystane dyke below
the path. Continue along the path to cross
the minor hillock of Bentie Knowe before
following a deer fence uphill. Go through
a gate to reach the top of Whitewisp Hill.

Turn right at the small cairn that marks
the summit, following a fence to traverse
a wide ridge towards Tarmangie Hill.
Straight ahead, the huge bulks of King's
Seat Hill, The Law, Andrew Gannel Hill
and Ben Cleuch line the horizon.

A gate in the fence leads to an obvious
track up to the two cairns at the summit

Ben Shee and Glensherup Reservoir from Scad Hill

of Tarmangie Hill. The second is the higher of the two and, at 645m, marks the highest point on the route.

Continuing westwards, the track leads back towards the fence. Do not cross the stile but follow the fence as it swings downhill to cross the head of Glen Sherup. Go through another gate, bearing right to climb the slopes of Scad Hill. The route doesn't go to the summit, but there is an obvious path to the left if you want to make the short detour.

A long straight path heads gently downhill from Scad Hill towards the rounded lump of Ben Shee. Stay on the main path to reach a drystane dyke. If you don't feel like tackling Ben Shee, there's a shortcut on the right just before the dyke, dropping down to the Glensherup

Reservoir before going through a gate and passing the Glensherup Fishery to reach the dam.

To continue over Ben Shee, go straight ahead, passing a sign to the summit. Just beyond the trees on the right, a rough track leaves the main path to lead steeply up to the flat top of the hill. Bear left just beyond the grassy circle and single stone that mark the summit to return to the main path, now a wide vehicle track.

Follow the track gradually downhill, eventually crossing a stile topped with a gate. Continue straight ahead, before turning right onto the access road for the Glensherup Fishery. At the reservoir, go through the gate to cross the dam. Climb the short incline on the far side to follow the outward track down to the car park.

Ben Shee

Distance **9.1km** Time **3 hours 15**
Terrain **hillside tracks, some steep**
Map **OS Explorer 366 or Harvey's
Superwalker XT25 'Ochil Hills'**
Access **no public transport to the start**

**This circular walk skirts around a
reservoir before climbing to the rounded
summit of Ben Shee, where there are fine
views to be admired. At 516m, Ben Shee
looms over the Glensherup and Lower
Glendevon Reservoirs. The name is from
the Gaelic word *sith* or *sidh* (pronounced
shee), meaning 'hill of the fairies'. In
Celtic mythology, *sithean* or *sidhean*
(pronounced *shee-an*) are often conical
hills, reputed to have hollow interiors
with the fairies dwelling inside.**

The walk begins at the Glen Sherup car
park. A path, signposted for the Ben Shee
Loop, leaves the northern end of the car
park and rises to join the wide forest
access track with towering conifer trees
lining both sides. The track climbs
gradually until Glensherup Reservoir
comes into view below.

The 12.3ha reservoir was built by
Dunfermline Corporation Water Works at
a cost of around £72,000. Opened in 1880
to supply drinking water to West Fife, it is
the smallest of the network of reservoirs
around Glen Devon. It is popular with
fishermen and is regularly stocked with
rainbow, blue and brown trout. The trout
are also popular with osprey, which can
often be seen hunting in the reservoir in
the summer.

A small path snakes down to a gate
before crossing the dam wall and
climbing to another gate on the far side.
Turn left to follow a rough road past
the little hut of the Glensherup Fishery
and to the right of a gate to cross a stile.
The path climbs steadily away from

◄ Looking towards the summit of Ben Shee

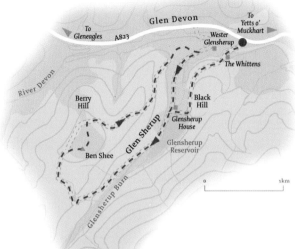

the reservoir for 1km before swinging sharply but briefly uphill by a drystane dyke and flattening out again. The views back across the reservoir from here are impressive.

After another 350m the path swings sharply around and climbs steadily to the brow of the hill, where there is a view to the Lower Glendevon Reservoir in the valley below. Joining a vehicle track, pass through a broken-down drystane dyke and continue uphill, passing a sign for the summit and bearing right at the fork.

As the trees to the right of the path come to an end, directly opposite Lower Glendevon Reservoir, a faint grassy track leaves the path and heads up to the top of the hill. The summit is marked by a single stone and a grassy circle. Continue straight across, bearing left to head down the hill.

At the bottom of the slope, turn right and continue gently downhill on a wide vehicle track to reach another stile. Beyond the stile, the track continues through a field, descending to meet a road. Turn right to follow the road to Glensherup House. Retrace your steps across the dam and back to the start of the walk.

Wether Hill

Distance **10.3km** Time **3 hours 30** Terrain **occasionally boggy or steep hill tracks** Map **OS Explorer 366 or Harvey's Superwalker XT25 'Ochil Hills'** Access **no public transport to the start**

Climb to the summits of two of the Ochils' lesser-known hills before returning along the old drover's road through Glen Eagles. Look out for the remains of various historic animal enclosure and rig and furrow farming systems scattered across the two hills.

The walk begins at a lay-by beyond a cattle grid on the private road leading to the Frandy Fishery and the Upper and Lower Glendevon Reservoirs.

Continue along the road, turning up a stony track just beyond a wooden chalet. Where the track veers left, continue straight ahead, following some grassy ATV tracks uphill.

Carry on along the ATV tracks past a small but picturesque lochan and onwards to the summit of Common Hill. From the summit, the track follows the line of the hillside high above the Lower Glendevon Reservoir.

The ATV tracks mostly disappear as you pick your way carefully across a fairly wet piece of ground between Common Hill and Wether Hill, though they can be seen occasionally. Pick them up again on the other side, climbing uphill towards the flat, rounded and

generally featureless summit of Wether Hill.

To the south, Ben Shee sits in front of Innerdownie, with Whitewisp, Tarmangie, King's Seat and Andrew Gannel Hills along the horizon. To the north, the view extends across Auchterarder to Strathearn and the peaks of the Southern Highlands.

From the summit, follow an obvious set of ATV tracks northeast, heading in the general direction of Auchterarder. Bear left to follow the tracks off the hill. At the bottom of the hill, go through a gate and follow the deer fence to reach two gates at the bottom right corner of the field. Go through the gate on the right. This is the old drove road through Glen Eagles, which leads through woodland before paralleling the line of the A823.

This was the official route that cattle drovers were supposed to use to cross the Ochils, passing through Glen Eagles and Glen Devon before paying a toll at Yetts o' Muckhart. However, the drovers were adept at avoiding tolls, finding other routes through the hills instead.

The road crosses a couple of fords before passing St Mungo's Farm. A short way beyond the farm, a natural spring which forms a large pool a little downhill of the path is known as St Mungo's Well. The connection with the saint is not known. After fording another three burns, you'll see a gate leading back onto the fisheries road. Turn right to cross the cattle grid and return to the start.

◂ The view down Glendevon from the slopes of Common Hill

67

The Frandy Reservoirs

Distance **9.1km** Time **2 hours 30**
Terrain **surfaced private road throughout
with some ascent** Map **OS Explorer 366 or
Harvey's Superwalker XT25 'Ochil Hills'**
Access **no public transport to the start**

**This easy walk follows a surfaced
road, which belongs to Scottish Water,
deep into the hills. The two reservoirs
on this route work in conjunction
with Glensherup, Glenquey and
Castlehill Reservoirs to supply water
to Dunfermline and West Fife. These
five reservoirs hold around 12.7 billion
litres of water between them.
Birdwatchers should look out for birds
of prey such as osprey, buzzards, hen
harrier, peregrine falcon and red kites
on the route.**

The walk begins at a lay-by beyond a
cattle grid on a private road, signposted

for the Frandy Fishery, just off the A823.
This is a private road and members of the
public should not drive up it.

Continue along the road on foot.
Rounding a corner, the grass-covered wall
of the Lower Glendevon Reservoir comes
into view. Pass the picturesque old
pumphouse, which dates from 1924,
perhaps stopping to wonder at the water
rushing down from the outlet at the top
of the dam, before following the road up
to the reservoir itself.

Lower Glendevon Reservoir, also known
as Lower Frandy Reservoir, was planned
by the Dunfermline Corporation Water
Works in 1912/13 and built by German
prisoners during the First World War.
It opened in 1924.

Walk along the side of the reservoir
for a while, passing a fishing lodge and
a jetty with rowing boats for hire. The

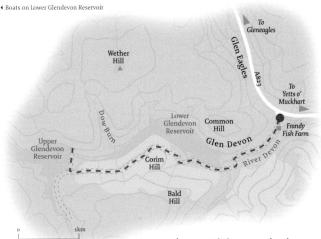

◄ Boats on Lower Glendevon Reservoir

reservoir is a popular fishing spot, and is regularly stocked with rainbow, brown and blue trout.

The road begins to climb away from the lower reservoir and soon reaches the Upper Glendevon Reservoir. Far later than its lower counterpart, this was originally built in 1955 to regulate the water stored in the first reservoir. It covered several significant archaeological sites, including a Bronze Age burial mound and several medieval settlements.

However, the dam suffered from significant leakage and concerns were raised about its stability. Despite repair work that was carried out in 1960, 1968

and 1975, restrictions were placed upon the reservoir's capacity, with the result that it was never more than half full for the first 35 years of its life. It was not until the early 1990s that a new strengthening project saw 280,000 cubic metres of rock placed in layers against the dam wall. After completion in 1994, the water level could finally be raised to the level intended four decades earlier. A further initiative saw a 264kW hydroelectric turbine installed in the watercourse running down to Lower Glendevon.

At the end of the road go through the gate immediately ahead, following the Scottish Rights of Way sign across the dam wall. Retrace your steps down to the start of the walk.

69

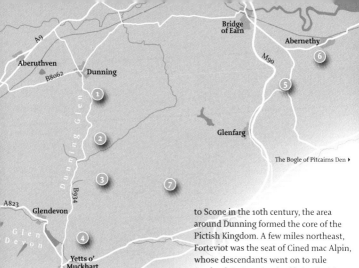

The Bogle of Pitcairns Den ▶

To the east of Glen Devon, the Ochil Hills become less rugged. The hills are thick with commercial forestry and offer few opportunities for walking.

Dunning was visited by the Romans when the troops of Septimius Severus built a huge camp at the town as they pressed north in their attempts to defeat the Maeatae. The camp is one of many stretching from Falkirk up the northeast of Scotland as far as the Moray Firth. A more permanent fort was built at Braco, a little to the west of here. The offensive ended with the genocide of the indigenous tribes in 210AD, only halted by the death of Severus in York in 211. The Maeatae hillfort above Glenearn was destroyed by the Romans as part of this campaign.

Before the centre of royal power shifted to Scone in the 10th century, the area around Dunning formed the core of the Pictish Kingdom. A few miles northeast, Forteviot was the seat of Cined mac Alpin, whose descendants went on to rule Scotland. In Dunning itself, the Pictish lordship ruled from the hillfort at Dun Knock. The magnificent Dupplin Cross, which once stood on the Gask Ridge overlooking Forteviot, is now housed in the town's St Serf's Church.

Like Glen Devon and Glen Eagles, Dunning Glen was used as a drove route across the Ochils, linking Muckhart in the south to Dunning in the north. At the southern end of the glen, the River Devon cascades out of the dam of Castlehill Reservoir to pass beneath an old bridge that carries the road, before turning southwest towards Crook of Devon.

Unfortunately, no public transport runs through Dunning Glen, so a vehicle is necessary for most of the walks in this chapter. The narrow B934 which leads through the secluded glen is much quieter than the busier route traversing Glen Devon.

Dunning Glen and the east

1 Pitcairns Den 72
A stunning riverside walk through
an ancient wooded glen

2 Knowehead Forest 74
Follow a forest road to a remote farm
on this peaceful walk

3 Innerdouny Hill 76
A straightforward walk to the
summit of this little hill

4 Lendrick Hill 78
A steep climb through woodland
to the summit of this dinky hill at
the southern end of Dunning Glen
is rewarded with fantastic views

5 Glenfarg Railway Tunnels 80
Make sure you have a good torch
with you for this pitch-dark tunnel
walk beneath the Ochil Hills

6 Abernethy Glen and Castle Law 82
From a mysterious medieval tower,
follow in the final footsteps of
condemned witches to the hilltop
where their coven was uncovered

7 Black Hill and the Butter Road 84
This short walk follows an old
right of way before circumnavigating
a small hill

Pitcairns Den

Distance **5.9km** Time **1 hour 30**
Terrain **country roads and forest tracks
with some ascent; one avoidable steep
climb** Map **OS Explorer 369**
Access **regular bus service to Dunning
from Perth and Auchterarder**

**Follow the Dunning Burn through an
ancient wooded glen in this delightful
riverside walk. Pitcairns Den is an
enchanting old woodland that has been
here for centuries. In the spring, it is
carpeted with bluebells. Among the
wildlife found here are roe deer and
red squirrels.**

The walk starts in front of St Serf's
Church in Dunning. St Serf was a 6th-
century Christian missionary who was
reputed to have slain a dragon which had
been terrorising the Pictish village of
Dunning. The church that bears his name

was built in around 1200, probably on the
site of a grove of thorn trees. It's worth
going inside to view the 9th-century
Dupplin Cross, a symbol of the power of
the Pictish royal family.

Head along Kirkstyle Square, following
the road towards Newton of Pitcairns.
After crossing a road called Dunning Park,
a track leads up the hill to the left, passing
a beacon on a pole erected in 1999 to bring
in the new millennium. This hill, Dun
Knock, was the site of a hillfort. It was
first identified as a series of concentric
crop marks in 1978. The woodland
contains further upstanding banks. The
fort has been dated to the late Bronze or
early Iron Age, although archaeologists
have found that the site has been a centre
of activity since Neolithic times. The old
Irish *dúnán*, meaning 'little fort', probably
gave the village its name.

◀ The Dunning Burn

Continue up and over the hill, descending steeply and bearing left to emerge through a gap in the fence. Go through a gate and turn left to follow the road up the hill for 200m, reaching a narrow stone gateway into the woodland.

Accompany the track through the trees. Continue straight ahead at a junction, following the sign for the 'Circuit of the Den' and bearing right to walk alongside the Dunning Burn as it tumbles through the glen.

The path crosses a couple of bridges, the second of which is named the 'Bogle Brig' after a wooden mask that was found nearby. The mask is nailed to a tree above the bridge.

The path leads uphill via a steep set of steps. If you want to avoid this steep climb and the upper path, retrace your steps along the outward route.

At the top of the hill, the path levels out and bears northwards along the hillside, offering occasional tantalising views of Strathearn through the trees, before dropping back to join the outward route.

Bear right along an old path to return to the road. Head downhill from here, turning left at the corner to follow a narrow lane down to meet the Dunning Burn again. Bear left to follow the burn back down into Dunning.

Entering the village, the route passes a thorn tree, commemorating the burning of the village on 28 January 1716 by Jacobites, following the Battle of Sheriffmuir. Thorn trees were sacred to the Gaelic-speaking pagan Picts who occupied Dunning in the 6th century. The old Gaelic for thorn tree is *drae-gen*, which brings us back to the dragon-slaying St Serf, and his church, just around the corner where the walk began.

73

Knowehead Forest

Distance **7.5km** Time **2 hours**
Terrain **easy if occasionally steep forest
vehicle track** Map **OS Explorer 369**
Access **no public transport to the start**

This is a very straightforward and
easy route, following a wide vehicle
track through commercial forestry
and looping around a lonely farm before
returning across open hillside. Although
the walk is waymarked with a yellow
arrow on a green background, the route
is obvious.

Begin at the gate to Greenhill and
Craigbaikie Forest, where there is space
for several cars to park. Return to the
road and head north for 350m to reach
a cottage.

This cottage, Blaeberry Toll, was the
former tollhouse on the Dunning Road.
The road between Dunning and the

Common of Dunning, a little to the south
of here, has been in use since the Middle
Ages and tolls were collected from
villagers taking their cattle for grazing on
the Common. The villagers bypassed the
toll by taking their cattle over Eldritch
Hill, behind the tollhouse, along a route
known as the Corb Road which, though
no longer in existence, has been
identified by archaeologists.

The signed entrance to Knowehead
Forest is opposite Blaeberry Toll. Go
around the gate, picking up a rough
surfaced farm access road which curves
gently up the hill, passing through a
mixture of mature forest and some young
trees. As the track rises, it passes, below
on the left, the former Blaeberry Hill
Curling Pond. Now covered in reeds, in
the mid-19th century this was home to
the Curlers of Dunning.

◄ Broadheadfold Farm

Bear left and left again at the next couple of junctions. Beyond a gate after the second junction, the track begins to swing around in a wide loop.

Broadheadfold Farm can be seen downhill on the right. The farm has been here since at least 1866, when it appeared on the first OS map of Perthshire.

The track swings around the farm, dropping quickly into the glen below, where a tributary of the Water of May runs along the valley floor with the

farmhouse now perched on the horizon high above.

Skirting around Long Hill, pass into a deep and picturesque glen, where tall trees are perched precariously on the very edge of a small scarp beside the track. Far below, the Water of May rolls gently through the glen.

Bear right to climb steeply up the hill and meet with the outward track, turning left to follow it back to the beginning of the walk.

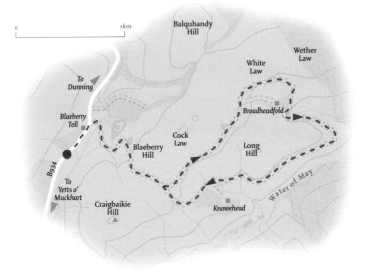

Innerdouny Hill

Distance **4.6km** Time **1 hour 45** Terrain **wide vehicle track for most of the route; grassy hill track; some ascent** Map **OS Explorer 369** Access **no public transport to the start**

At 497m, Innerdouny is a great little hill. Not to be confused with the better known and much bigger Innerdownie in Glen Devon, this is an easy walk up a wide vehicle access road before climbing a gentle hill track to the summit.

The derivation of the name is the same as for Innerdownie: from the Gaelic *Inbhir*, meaning 'confluence', and *dùnaigh*, 'hillfort', probably in reference to the fort on nearby Down Hill.

The walk begins in Littlerigg car park

on the B934. Cut around the gate and follow a wide access road as it first swings around Little Rig hill before climbing Muckle Rig. The names of both Little Rig and Muckle Rig are from the Scots word *Rig*, meaning 'hill crest'.

Bear right at a fork, ignoring the waymarker hidden in the long grass and descending slightly to cross the Back Burn before climbing the slope of Brunt Hill, a shoulder of Innerdouny Hill.

Looking back from here, the eastern flanks of the hills around Glen Devon and the Hillfoots can be seen: Innerdownie, Ben Shee, Tarmangie and Ben Cleuch, as well as the Glendevon Reservoirs.

Just beyond a lay-by, the track swings around to the northeast side of the hill and drops slightly before entering the

◂ Innerdownie Hill dominates the view back down the track

woodland of the tree-covered slopes of Innerdouny Hill. The sitka spruce trees are enormous here and it is easy to feel dwarfed by them.

The track climbs through the trees across another shoulder of Innerdouny Hill called Scowling Craig Hill. The spruce give way to much smaller native trees such as Scots pine. The trees eventually disappear altogether at a firebreak which is perhaps 100m across. Coalcraigy Hill is to the east and the Lomond Hills can be seen on the horizon.

Continue to the end of the firebreak where an old broken-down fence borders the edge of the forest. Turn off uphill

here, following a rough and sometimes muddy track along the line of the fence.

Pass through a gap in an old drystane dyke, following the track away from the fence and around a small clump of trees to reach the trig point at the summit.

There is an excellent view from this hilltop. Loch Leven can be seen to the east, and Fife and Kinross to the southeast. King's Seat, Innerdownie and Ben Shee dominate the western horizon, while Auchlinsky Hill and Seamab Hill sit behind Down Hill.

There is no way down from Innerdouny Hill other than to retrace your steps to the car park.

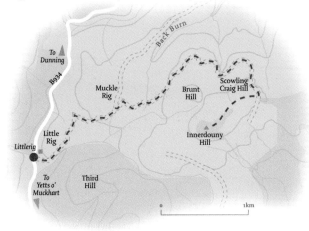

Lendrick Hill

Distance **5.1km** Time **1 hour 30**
Terrain **good vehicle track, forest tracks,
grassy hilltop path; the slopes are steep
and covered in moss and can become
extremely slippery when wet**
Map **OS Explorer 369** Access **no public
transport to the start**

At 456m, Lendrick Hill is one of the
smaller peaks in the Ochils, but the steep
climb up its slopes is rewarded with
terrific views from the summit. Lendrick
is derived from the Brythonic *Llanerch*,
meaning 'clear space' or 'glade'. This is
not in evidence today – the hill is largely
cloaked in the commercial forestry
plantation of Lendrick Forest.

This partially waymarked circuit
approaches the hill by a forest vehicle
track. Access to the summit is gained by
a couple of firebreaks which cut through
the trees.

The route begins at a gate by the
entrance to a rough vehicle track from the
B934, beside a signpost to Lendrick Hill.
Go around the gate and follow the vehicle
track up the hill and into Lendrick Forest.

As you ascend there are views behind
you towards Seamab Hill, Auchlinsky Hill
and Whitewisp Hill. In the immediate
foreground, Down Hill, with its crown of
Iron Age fortifications, sits in front of
Innerdownie. After a hairpin S-bend, the
track becomes rougher. A small cairn by

the roadside offers a laborious and gruelling route to the summit, but it is best ignored in favour of the less arduous alternative a few hundred metres along the track.

At a waymarker, follow a damp, moss-covered path uphill through a firebreak in the trees. Initially steep and slippery, the path swings through the forest to climb gradually, continuing upwards at another waymarker to finally escape from the trees.

A grassy path leads to a stile and continues towards the summit, which is marked by a cairn and a trig point about 100m away. To the east, there are fantastic views across Loch Leven to East and West Lomond and, to the south, Fife and the River Forth stretch out towards the distant Pentlands. To the west, the hills of southern Glen Devon dominate the scene.

From the cairn, turn left to head down the hillside, aiming for a wide firebreak and the corner of a low fence. Step over the fence, and head down the steep moss- and grass-covered slope of the firebreak. As on the way up, this slope can become very slippery in the wet.

At the bottom of the hill step over a narrow ditch to return to the vehicle track. Turn left to follow the track back down to the car park.

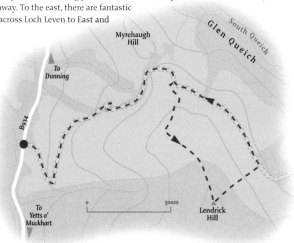

◀ The sun rises over the summit of Lendrick Hill

Glenfarg Railway Tunnels

Distance **8.4km** Time **2 hours 15**
Terrain **unsurfaced tracks; minor country
roads; some ascent** Map **OS Explorer 369**
Access **no public transport to the start**

**This fascinating walk along a
dismantled railway line is not for the
claustrophobic or nyctophobic. The
railway line through Glenfarg was
opened by the North British Railway in
1890, at the same time as the Forth
Bridge, and carried the line from
Edinburgh via Kinross to Perth. At
Glenfarg it went through two tunnels
beneath the Ochil Hills, each nearly
500m long.**

Although it escaped the Beeching cuts
of the mid-1960s, the line was closed in
1970. Today, the two tunnels can be
walked, although they are pitch dark and
you should carry a good-quality torch.

Begin at the car park of the Bein Inn.

You should report to the hotel reception
before beginning the walk if leaving a
car here and pay a small deposit (which
can be redeemed against refreshments in
the inn when you return).

Turn left out of the car park and walk
along the road. After 250m, opposite the
entrance to the Binn Ecopark, turn left
down a surfaced path and climb the hill
beyond to cross a bridge over a railway
cutting. The track curves right. Bear right
through a gate, descending to turn left
onto the old railway.

Go along the track, quickly reaching the
Northern Tunnel. The 460m tunnel curves
beneath the hillside. Look out for
hideaways built into the walls for workers
to take refuge from passing trains.

Emerging from the tunnel, enjoy the
panorama of the Braes of the Carse to the
left. Bear left at a fork to descend to the
foot of the Kilnockie Viaduct, which

◄ Glenfarg tunnels

carried the railway over the Baiglie Burn. Turn left up a vehicle track between two ruined cottages and continue straight ahead at a junction to follow the track to the top of the hill before turning left onto a minor country road.

The road rises to cross a bridge over the M90. After the railway was closed, its former route became the route of the motorway.

The road meanders along for a little, shadowing the motorway in the cutting below and climbing up and over a hill. Turn left at a sign for Meikle Fieldie, crossing the M90 again by another bridge, and turn right at the far side to go down the road towards the farm.

Just before reaching the farm, turn right opposite the first shed, going through a gate and follow the farm track which winds down the hill. Bear left through two gates at the bottom, continuing downhill along a pleasant woodland track beside a burn.

Exiting the woodland at a gate, turn left to walk northwards along the B996, which runs alongside the old railway line

beyond the fence on the right. Turn onto the old railway line after 150m, continuing northwards through a cutting and crossing a viaduct over the road to reach the entrance to the South Tunnel. This tunnel is slightly longer and straighter than the northern one and, although it is dark, you can always see the tunnel mouth at one end or the other.

At the far end, pass beneath the bridge that you crossed at the start of the walk before turning left up the track that you came down earlier to go over the bridge and return to the start.

81

Abernethy Glen and Castle Law

Distance **4.6km** Time **1 hour 45**
Terrain **rough hill and woodland
tracks, minor country roads; some
steep climbs** Map **OS Explorer 370**
Access **regular bus service to Abernethy
from Perth and Glenrothes**

**The historic village of Abernethy was
once the capital of the Pictish kingdom.
At its centre is an 11th-century Irish-style
roundtower – one of only two such towers
in Scotland. The Treaty of Abernethy, in
which Malcolm III of Scotland swore
allegiance to William the Conqueror in
return for estates in Cumbria, was
signed near the tower in 1072.**

Starting at the foot of Abernethy Round
Tower, return to the main road. Turn left,
crossing to head up Kirk Wynd.

The road soon leaves the village, quickly
becoming a rough vehicle track. Continue
uphill, following the signs for Abernethy
Glen. Where the road disappears through a
gate, take the track which eases up the hill.

This is the Witches' Road. The road is
so called because a coven of 22 witches
was marched this way to Abernethy Hill
in 1625, where they were burned to death.

Drop down a set of steps to walk along
the banks of the Ballo Burn, following
the sign for Craigden.

Reaching a minor country road, turn
right to climb gently uphill. Just beyond
the 30mph signs, take the path signed
for Castle Law.

The path rises steeply but steadily,
becoming a gentler climb beyond a
crosspaths. Passing an information board,
bear left to climb sharply up to the
shattered remains of an ancient hillfort.
A cairn marks the summit of the hill.

The origins of the fort are unknown.

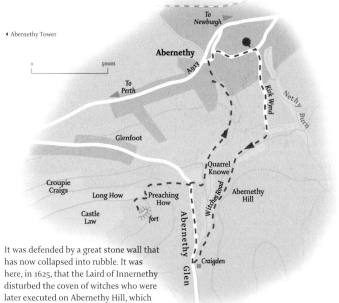

◄ Abernethy Tower

It was defended by a great stone wall that has now collapsed into rubble. It was here, in 1625, that the Laird of Innernethy disturbed the coven of witches who were later executed on Abernethy Hill, which can be seen to the east.

The view north from here is superb. Abernethy sits in the shadow of the hill, while further north the River Earn joins the River Tay before flowing into the Firth of Tay. The Sidlaws, a continuation of the Ochils, rise beyond the river. Dundee and the Tay Bridge can be seen in the east while, on a clear day, the view north extends as far as the Cairngorms.

To return, retrace your steps back down to the road. Go straight across and through a gate on the other side, following a narrow track down to the Ballo Burn again. The burn drops away from the path, but just before a gate, turn down a

set of steps to meet with it once again.

Continue straight ahead beyond another gate, following a wide track between two wire fences. Enter woodland beyond a kissing gate, dropping down steps to cross the burn at a bridge. Here you are level with the burn, which gurgles along pleasantly beside the path.

Cross the burn again at another bridge, climbing slightly to turn right onto a narrow road, and taking this back down into the village to arrive opposite the Nurse Peattie Memorial Garden.

Turn right, crossing the burn at a stone bridge, and keeping right to follow Abernethy Main Street back to the tower.

Black Hill and the Butter Road

Distance **3.4km** Time **1 hour**
Terrain **mostly wide forestry access road,
some rough forest tracks with mild
ascent** Map **OS Explorer 369**
Access **no public transport to the start**

This short walk meanders through a
large forest with some spectacular views
across the eastern Ochils. The path,
which leads around the small tree-clad
summit of Black Hill, is very easy to
follow and poses no challenges.

The route begins in a large lay-by
with two gates and a stile, on a sharp
corner of the minor road between Path of
Condie and Milnathort. To get here, drive
north along North Street in Milnathort,
crossing the M90 and turning left. After

2.5km, turn right at a crossroads and
follow the minor road for a further 4km to
the lay-by, just south of Stronachie.

Cross the stile and follow the stony
vehicle access road on the left which leads
gradually up the hill into the forest. This
route is part of the ancient Butter Road.
Local tradition says it was used by the
monks of Culross Abbey to supply butter
to the royal court at Scone. Another story
is that it was used to reach shielings
where butter was made. A third
explanation is that it is an ancient drove
road and that the name is derived from
the Gaelic *bothar*, simply meaning 'road'.

Bear left to follow a road, then right to
head through a wide firebreak. The path
quickly deteriorates into a narrow, damp,

rough grass track. Follow the track straight through the firebreak to emerge, after 500m or so, onto the corner of another road.

Continue up the hill, following the road as it circles the summit of Black Hill. There are several benches dotted along the path on this stretch of the route – ideally placed to stop and enjoy the fantastic view across the eastern Ochils towards Innerdouny Hill, Coalcraigie Hill and, on the horizon, Innerdownie. To the south, Clackmannanshire and Fife stretch out towards the Forth and Grangemouth.

Tinto Hill, in the Borders, can be seen in the distance. Completists might be tempted to follow the vague path that climbs through a firebreak towards the small forest clearing near the summit of the hill, but, being surrounded by trees, it's really not worth the effort.

The road descends to meet with the Butter Road again. Turn left to return to the beginning of the walk.

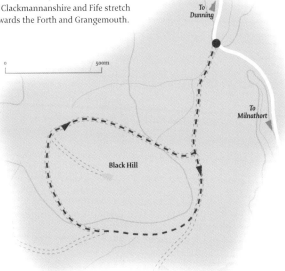

To
Dunning

0   500m

To
Milnathort

Black Hill

◄ Looking west from Black Hill towards distant Innerdownie

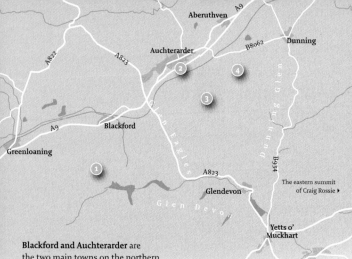

The eastern summit
of Craig Rossie ▶

Blackford and Auchterarder are the two main towns on the northern edge of the Ochils. At one time a road connected the two but both were bypassed when the A9 was built between Stirling and Perth in 1983.

The hills on this northern side of the Ochils sit on top of a huge aquifer, from which a springwater bottling plant in Blackford sources its water. It can take up to 15 years for water to filter from the top of the hills into the aquifer. The luxury Gleneagles Hotel and Golf Course sits between the two towns. Built by the Caledonian Railway Company, it opened in June 1924.

The Jacobites were the victims of many atrocities during the Uprisings of the early 18th century, but they committed one of their own in these towns between Stirling and Perth. After the Battle of Sheriffmuir in November 1715, the Jacobite army had retreated to Perth. Receiving information that a large Government force was advancing towards them in pursuit, they opted for a scorched earth policy, denying the approaching army food and shelter. Auchterarder was torched on the night of 24 January 1716, with only the church spared. The Jacobites then moved on to Blackford, where they repeated the exercise. Only two buildings survived.

Two nights later, they arrived in Crieff, where locals were told that the town was to be spared and only accommodation was required. But at a pre-set time, the troops rose and set the town ablaze, finishing the job by demolishing the bridge over the River Earn.

Shortly after Crieff, Dunning and Muthill suffered the same fate. Farms and other outlying buildings were also destroyed in what turned out to be a pointless act. As the Government troops approached, the Highlanders left Perth and scattered back to their homes.

Blackford and Auchterarder

1 Kinpauch Hill   88
This easy climb to a summit south
of Blackford is rewarded with
stunning views of the Highlands

2 Provost's Walk   90
Explore Auchterarder in this
surprisingly rural circuit around
the Lang Toon

3 Cloan Glen   92
A relaxing riverside amble through
a wooded glen

4 Craig Rossie   94
This circular walk climbs gently
to approach Craig Rossie from the
south, taking in a mysterious Pictish
fort on the way

Kinpauch Hill

Distance **8.3km** Time **3 hours**
Terrain **rough vehicle track, grassy hill track** Map **OS Explorer 366 or Harvey's Superwalker XT25 'Ochil Hills'**
Access **regular bus service to Blackford from Perth and Stirling. It is necessary to cross the busy A9. If driving, this can be avoided by parking on the minor road by the sign for Tillicoultry**

The climb to the top of Kinpauch Hill is rewarded with a stunning vista right across the Highland Boundary Fault from Ben Lomond in the west to the Sidlaw Hills in the east. The name of Kinpauch Hill seems to be derived from Gaelic, with *Ceann* meaning 'end', but the origin of *-pauch* is unknown.

With your back to the war memorial at Blackford's western end, turn left to head out of the village, passing the Tullibardine Distillery, where the smell of whisky lingers in the air.

Tullibardine began as a brewery. According to local legend, the beer they produced was a favourite of James IV, and the brewery was granted a Royal Charter in 1503. The brewery continued to produce beer until 1949, when it was converted into a distillery. The distillery draws its water from the Danny Burn, which rises on the northern slopes of Blairdenon before flowing through Glen Anny and downwards into Blackford and then converging with the Allan Water. At 8km, it is the longest burn in the western Ochils.

Carefully cross the A9 and turn left onto the very minor country road opposite. Cross the stile at the gate signed for

◄ View from the cairn at the summit

Tillicoultry and follow the rough-surfaced road which heads straight for the hill.

This was a former drove road that stretched between Blackford and Tillicoultry. When the mills of Tillicoultry were at their peak, the route was used by millworkers from Blackford to get to their place of work. These days it is a popular walking route between the two villages.

Go straight across two crossroads and bear left at a fork. The road becomes steeper as it swings into the Glen of Kinpauch. Here, the path is lined with heather, bracken, gorse and broom, and the Glen Burn weaves down the floor of the valley below. It is well worth looking over your shoulder, where the great pyramid of Ben Vorlich is framed by the steep sides of the glen.

At the top of the glen, just before a broken-down old gate, the path doubles back on itself to zigzag up the hill in a couple of switchbacks. Just before another gate, continue up the hill, following the fence before bearing left to take a grassy ATV track towards the summit.

Continue over the summit to the small cairn which lies a few hundred metres beyond. In the foreground of the sweeping outlook, Blackford nestles at the foot of the hill beyond the busy A9, and across Strathearn Crieff marks the beginning of the Highlands. All of the major mountains of the Southern

Highlands can be seen, including Ben Lomond, the Arrochar Alps, Ben Ledi, Stùc a'Chroin, Ben Vorlich, Ben More, Ben Lawers and Schiehallion. Carry on past the cairn for a gentle descent through the heather, rejoining the outward route and returning to Blackford.

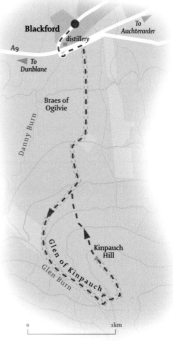

Provost's Walk

Distance **4.4km** Time **1 hour 15**
Terrain **formal paths, woodland tracks,
minor ascents** Map **OS Explorer OL47**
Access **regular bus service to
Auchterarder from Perth and Stirling**

Auchterarder's Provost's Walk is named
after Provost T E Young, who extended
an existing footpath across Auchterarder
Golf Course in the 1930s. He wanted a
walking route that was near the town
but felt as if it was in the countryside.
Nearly a century later, his vision is still
evident. The route has recently been
renovated and upgraded with signposts,
benches, solar lighting and mostly
surfaced paths.

Turn right out of the Crown Inn Wynd
car park in the middle of Auchterarder,
and follow the town's famously long High
Street downhill, turning right again onto
Abbey Road.

Just before an old bridge carries the
road across Ruthven Water, take the lane
opposite the entrance to Glenruthven
Mill, following the river as it bubbles
contentedly alongside. The Ruthven
Water rises in Glen Eagles and flows
north for 15km, joining the River Earn
near Aberuthven.

Bear left, passing Milton House. In the
19th century, a dyeworks stood opposite
the house, powered by the Ruthven Water.
Eventually the path reaches a bridge
where the river flows under the A9 and
over a fish ladder.

Head straight across the junction,
following the Jubilee Walk. The path runs

◀ The fish ladder on Ruthven Water

parallel to the A9, just on the other side of a hedge here, and the traffic can be quite noisy.

Bear left again along a rough surfaced track, still following Jubilee Walk, to descend into woodland. Go straight over the crosspaths and climb a set of steps to turn left at the next crosspaths, following the sign for Auchterarder Golf Course.

At the next junction, ignore the path that leads off down the hill and continue straight ahead, passing into woodland. Bear right at the next two forks, eventually arriving at a rough surfaced driveway.

Turn right through a metal gate into Primrose Park and climb the hill to follow a path to the left around the park, passing a play area and exiting through the gate onto Western Road. Continue along the road to return to the start of the walk.

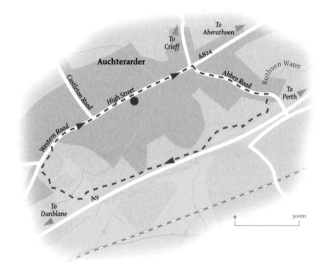

Cloan Glen

Distance **10km** Time **2 hours 45**
Terrain **surfaced roads, good forest and
hillside tracks, some moderate ascent**
Map **OS Explorer OL47** Access **regular bus
to Auchterarder from Perth and Stirling**

**The road through Cloan Glen forms
the northernmost part of the Cadgers'
Way, the beautiful old drove road
between Auchterarder and Dollar.**

Starting at the top of Abbey Road,
towards the eastern end of Auchterarder's
famously long High Street, follow Abbey
Road down to cross a bridge over the
Ruthven Water and then the A9.

Turn right, following a minor road as it
first sweeps southwest, then southeast to
pass beneath the railway. This is the
Stirling to Perth Line, opened by the

Scottish Central Railway in 1848. West
of the railway bridge was the site of
Auchterarder Railway Station, which was
closed in 1956.

Straight ahead, the Scottish Baronial
towers of Cloan House sit high on the
hillside. Built in 1852, it was home to
the Haldane family until 2015. Over the
years, it was visited by many
distinguished guests, including J M
Barrie, John Buchan and Julian Huxley.
A dog belonging to Barrie is buried in the
castle's seven-acre garden.

In the autumn of 1942, Archibald
Haldane became curious about the
history of the Cadgers' Way, which runs
beside the house. His research led to the
publication, eight years later, of his classic
text *The Drove Roads of Scotland*.

Rounding a sharp corner by a huge farmshed, take the road to Coulshill. Bear left at the fork and then, after around 250m, leave the road where a track drops into Cloan Glen to the right of the gates of Cloan House. Soon you are walking along a beautiful woodland track amongst elm, spruce and sycamore trees. The Cloan Burn accompanies the path.

A ford across the burn is bypassed by a set of wooden steps which lead to a bridge by a little waterfall further along.

Look out for an impressive waterfall hiding behind the trees to the right, where the Maller Burn joins the Cloan.

From here, the path climbs high above the burn, presently arriving back on the Coulshill road again. Follow the road downhill for a little before turning right to cross a stile at a sign for Auchterarder.

The rough and occasionally muddy path soon joins a grassy ATV track, quickly climbing above the glen and passing a tumbledown wooden barn.

Passing Bellshill Farm, turn right onto a stony vehicle track, crossing a couple of cattle grids and going straight over a crossroads to head down the hill towards Auchterarder.

Briefly join the outward route again to go beneath the railway, following the very minor road straight ahead at the next junction, signed for Auchterarder.

An underpass leads beneath the A9 to a crosspaths where the Ruthven Water tumbles over a fish ladder. Continue straight ahead, turning downhill at the top of Ruthven Street to return to the beginning of the walk.

◀ A tumbledown wooden shed above Cloan Glen

Craig Rossie

Distance **7.5km** Time **2 hours 45**
Terrain **easy-going vehicle track initially,
steep hill tracks thereafter**
Maps **OS Explorer 369 and OL47**
Access **no public transport to the start**

**This small but steep hill is often seen
as the jewel in the crown of the northern
Ochils, and a climb to its rounded, grassy
summit is rewarded with spectacular
views. Rising suddenly to a height of
410m from the flat lands of Strathearn
between Auchterarder and Dunning,
Craig Rossie is volcanic in origin. The
Romans had a huge camp at Dunning,
a few miles to the east, and its name is
probably Latin in origin, in reference to
its red-hued basalt rocks.**

The walk starts at the beginning of the
track to Pairney Farm, just off the B8062.
There is very limited parking here, and
care should be taken not to block any
of the gates. Alternatively, there is
room to park on the verge a little west
of the entrance.

Go through the gate and follow the
track past the farm, climbing gently
before levelling out at a disused quarry.
Another gate marks the entrance to
picturesque Pairney Glen, with Pairney
Burn running along the glen floor.
The road climbs quickly along the
glen, with the turbines on the summit
of Steele's Knowe lining the horizon to
the southwest.

Where the track ahead is blocked by a
gate, bear left, leaving the road in 200m to
follow a grassy ATV track directly up and
go straight over the unremarkable summit
of Beld Hill. Continue towards Ben Effrey,
the prominent summit on the left.

An Iron Age fort once stood on Ben

◀ The hillfort on Ben Effrey

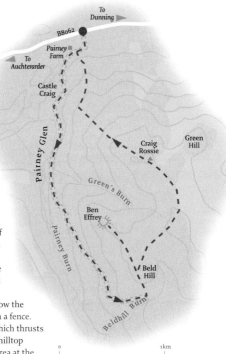

Effrey, and the surviving earthworks can clearly be seen. Aged between 1500 and 2500 years old, the fort is a Scheduled Ancient Monument. With steep or precipitous slopes on three of its four sides, it could only be approached from the south, where further defence in the form of a huge wall protected the fort's inhabitants.

The summit is marked by a small cairn. The twin peaks of Craig Rossie are visible to the east, but the deep glen of Green's Burn is as impassable now as it was when it formed part of the fort's defences.

Return to Beld Hill and follow the ATV tracks eastwards to reach a fence. Turn towards Craig Rossie, which thrusts suddenly upwards from this hilltop plateau. Cross a brief boggy area at the foot of the hill, and take the short but steep track to the trig point on the hill's eastern summit.

The view to the northwest overlooks Auchterarder and Strathearn to the Highland Boundary Fault beyond Crieff. Ben Cleuch can be seen to the southwest and West Lomond to the southeast. Dunning lies to the east, while the Sidlaw Hills in Angus are in the northeast.

The track continues over a small dip, passing the cairn on the western summit before dropping quite steeply down the hill towards a gate at the corner of a fence. Turn right beyond the gate, following the fence for a while before swinging downhill towards Pairney Farm. Returning to the farm, follow the road back to the beginning of the walk.

95

Index

Abernethy Glen	82
Abbey Craig	8
Allan Water	14, 22
Alva	28, 30, 32
Andrew Gannel Hill	36
Ashfield	22
Auchlinsky Hill	54, 56
Auchterarder	90, 92
Bank Hill	44
Ben Buck	30
Ben Cleuch	30, 36
Ben Effrey	94
Ben Ever	30
Ben Shee	62, 64
Ben Thrush	60
Black Hill	84
Blackford	86
Blairdenon	18
Blairlogie	12
Bridge of Allan	14, 16
Cadger's Gate	46
Cadgers' Way	46, 60, 92
Cadgers' Yett	60
Castle Campbell	42, 44, 46, 48
Castlehill Reservoir	54, 56, 58
Cloan Glen	92
Common Hill	66
Commonedge Hill	56
Craig Rossie	94
Crook of Devon	52
Darn Road, The	14
Devon, River	38, 40, 52
Dollar	38, 40, 42, 44, 46, 48
Dumyat	10, 12, 26
Dunblane	14, 16, 20, 22
Dunning	72
Gathering Stone, The	20
Glen Devon	54
Glen Eagles	66
Glen Quey	46, 58
Glen Road, The	16
Glen Sherup	62, 64
Glendevon	46, 54, 56, 58, 60
Glenfarg	80
Greenforet Hill	18
Hillfoot Hill	48
Innerdouny Hill	76
Innerdownie	58, 62
Kilnockie Viaduct	80
King's Seat Hill	36, 44
Kinpauch Hill	88
Kippenrait Glen	14, 16
Knowehead Forest	74
Law, The	36
Lendrick Hill	78
Lossburn Reservoir	10, 26
Lower Glendevon Reservoir	64, 66, 68
MacRae Monument	20
Menstrie Glen	26
Mickle Corum	18
Mill Glen	34, 36
Muckhart Mill	40
Ochil Hills Woodland Park	32
Pitcairns Den	72
Provost's Walk	90
Rumbling Bridge Gorge	52
Saddle Hill	44
Seamab Hill	56
Sheriffmuir	18, 20
Silver Glen	30
Steele's Knowe	60
Tarmangie Hill	44, 62
Tillicoultry	34, 36, 38
Tormaukin Hotel	46, 58, 60
Upper Glendevon Reservoir	68
Wallace Monument	8
Wether Hill	66
Whitewisp Hill	44, 62